AT HALF-PAST EIGHT

❧ AT ❧
HALF-PAST EIGHT
ESSAYS OF THE THEATRE 1921-1922
By
JAMES AGATE

BENJAMIN BLOM  New York/London

First Published 1923
Reissued 1969 by
Benjamin Blom, Inc., Bronx, New York 10452
and 56 Doughty Street, London, W.C. 1

Library of Congress Catalog Card Number 70-91308

Printed in the United States of America

Contents

	PAGE
VOLUNTARY	11
MARIE LLOYD	29
THREE PLAYS OF IBSEN	35
HAIL PUNCH, AND FAREWELL!	47
A LANCE FOR JANE	55
ART AND THE SCREEN	63
DEAR BARRIE	69
TWO WAYS OF BEING EARNEST	75
ANOTHER ESSAY ON THE COMIC SPIRIT	80
MARY QUEEN OF DRINKWATER	96
A SERMON TO COMMUNISTS	108
THE NEW IMMORALITY	113
THREE PERIODS	118
GENTLE IS AS GENTILE DOESN'T	134
MAB AND HER FRIENDS	139
A NEW PERCY BALLAD	144
SOME FILM-EMOTIONS AND A MORAL	149
A LITTLE POT OF JELLY	163
ANY CHILD'S PLAY	168
SOME FOREIGN PLAYS	174
THE CENCI	186
IN THE PIT	192
A SPECTACLE FOR SPECTACLES	201
MAIDS, YOUR TOAST!	207
WEST OF SUEZ	212
THE WAY OF A GOOSE	218
IAGO'S ANCESTRESS	223
METAPHYSICS AND MELODRAMA	228
FLIGHTS THAT FAILED	233

5

to
Filson Young
A restorer of bygone glories

Note

THE TWO ESSAYS ON THE ART OF the screen are not intended to be more than tentative. When they first appeared it was suggested on the one hand that their claim for consideration of the film as an art was altogether too sweeping; on the other, that this pretention had long been relegated to the limbo of accepted things. I have written of the screen as I have found it—a medium devoid, or almost devoid, of art in actual practice, but one capable of immense artistic development. The critic should not be prejudiced against the possibilities of the cinema merely because nine-tenths of present-day films are adaptations from maudlin, tenth-rate novels possessing no artistic significance. It was a French scientist who reconstructed a perfectly serious animal from a single funny-bone; and it should be possible for us equally to reconstruct the glories of the English novel from the inane phantasmagoria of our present-day best-sellers, or to foretell a future for this infant art.

The screen seems to me to be already sufficiently hampered by its association with vulgar American producers. It should not be shackled, at the moment, with the imposition of rigid rules and narrow laws. The dramatic critic will do well to content himself, for the time being, with throwing a lenient and a friendly glance at it as occasion serves.

9

Voluntary

T is difficult to understand the show of reluctance with which your dramatic critic garners his sheaves. The present stacking is my third; and this preliminary essay, which for a reason presently to appear I have called "Voluntary," is its thatch.

The reluctant parade is pure humbug. There is a passage in a comedy by Mr. Henry Arthur Jones in which the arch-reasoner rounds on the arch-scapegrace something after this fashion:

"Do you mean to tell me, boy, that you do not entertain for Mrs. Blank a passionate, bodily desire?"

"I give you my word of honour, sir, that I do not."

"Then why the devil don't you?"

Not the exact words perhaps, but the gist. I can still hear the emphasis which Henry Neville put into that last line, and watch his right arm saw the air; yet not with such violence as to disturb the button-hole in that left lapel which he kept so carefully presented to the audience. I shall never be persuaded that Neville was not a better actor than Wyndham, whom I saw but twice: in *David Garrick*, in which he croaked throughout like some melancholy frog, and in *Rosemary*, wherein he played an old man of ninety with the plump hands of twenty-three. It is, perhaps, unfair to judge an unromantic actor in romantic parts, and they tell me that Wyndham was at his best in simulations of the natural.

Voluntary

Well, seeing's believing, and as I never saw Wyndham attempt the natural—Torvald Helmer, shall I say, or the Rev. James Mavor Morell—I have no opinion on the point. One is a little sceptical as to the amount of naturalism to be got by any actor into so romantic a part as Sir Christopher Deering or Sir Daniel (Mr. Justice) Carteret. Can it be that Wyndham owed his success with the British public to the fact that he was prosaic in presentation of the romantic, and romantic in portrayal of the natural? I shall never believe that Sir Charles's containment and measure, if indeed these qualities were his, could have given me the same ecstasy as Neville's untempered flamboyance. Unashamedly magnificent, the characters of this stagiest of actors hang for ever on the walls of memory, the master-oleographs of his time.

Why the devil, I would ask with some of Neville's impatience, should dramatic critics be ashamed to avow the passionate, almost sensual and perfectly natural desire to see themselves a second time in print? Do we really exhume our old notices with misgiving? I believe this pretence to be as silly as the deprecation in the morning of the work one did overnight. " Hot air and dust of the playhouse were still in your lungs; you were sure to say things that would seem sorry gush or rant if you saw them again in the morning." If you saw them again in the morning! As if one didn't prop them up against the coffee-pot and pore over them, and note the roughnesses which only need a little smoothing down, and the stupidities which, alas! ought not to be there at all, and come finally to the conclusion that with time to file and polish the thing isn't so bad after all. Why the

Voluntary

devil should it be bad in the case of those critics who can give the best part of a week and the whole of their heart and soul and brain to their lucubrations ? Work achieved in these conditions which is not worth reading twice was not worth writing once. Clap into't roundly, is my advice to all good critics debating the question of reprinting. Hesitancy is no other than the hawking and spitting which the little page declared to be the prologue to a bad voice. And if your wavering proceeds from a doubt as to the ultimate value of your pronouncements—why then, let me tell you, sir, that your qualms are something late in the day, that this is a matter which should have been resolved or ever you put pen to paper. I have no sympathy with the artist who looks upon everything that he has made, and, behold, it is very bad. Republish, then, with a bold front; republish and be damned.

For damned you will be, of a certainty. Writers in the same line will never get on together better than bishops of different shades of gaiters. I suppose that we all think more or less the same thing about the plays which it is our happiness or misery to behold; the difference is in the manner of our expression. Well do I remember how a distinguished writer hovered, throughout a whole column, over my last book of the theatre, brushing it now with this wing of compliment, now with that. Finally he pounced: declaring that while he found in the book many things which he himself might have said, he did not think that he would —oh, most decidedly he knew that he would not—have said them in quite the same way. There was that about this judgment which filled me with the acutest dolor. This fellow, said the writer in effect, is as a clumsy bull trampling under foot all that bric-à-brac which, to a person of my taste, is the theatre. The one exquisite critic who, vowing he would ne'er reprint, has ne'er reprinted, is Mr. Max Beerbohm; at whom I would hurl reproach after the manner of the old actor flinging his voice against the gallery wall, even as far as distant Rapallo. For exquisiteness is the one test to which all writing on the theatre must be brought at last, and I hold it vile economy that he who has the greatest store of that perfection should be the chariest in its display.

In the practical business of life there is little need for literary airs and graces. I do not desire that my plumber shall make phrases; I desire simply that he shall plumb. When I would till my garden I am not displeased that my ironmonger should reply "Re esteemed enquiry for Spades. Best quality, 7s. 6d. Cheaper grade, 4s. 6d. Trusting to receive esteemed order, Ploughman and Hogg." Such a communication delights me; it has all the directness and simplicity of an inscription for a public building. I feel that Messrs. Ploughman and Hogg are good fellows whom it would be pleasant to know, whereas I desire no acquaintance of him who offers me boots under the name of Foot-Joy, or pyjamas disguised as Slumber-Wear.

In the world of the theatre you must use a trifle of elegance. You cannot say of a play that it has a stout sole or is guaranteed not to shrink. You can say that it is a good play, or a bad play, or one which seems to you both good and bad, or half-way between the two. The point is that the critic's duty is more than the awarding

Voluntary

of marks, the assigning of places in a class. In a railway-table all that we demand is accuracy and clearness of type. " Stops to take up " is a phrase which I fault, not on the score of elegance, but because it does not tell me whether the visitor whom I am expecting may descend. In an account of a play or piece of acting we are entitled to demand more than exactness of information. We are to demand that the critic shall declare his formula for beauty, explicit as that piece of platinum which, at the Standard Office, defines the unit of the pound; and that to that declared formula he shall refer his judgments. The critic may retort that this is all very well, but that the play is not over before eleven o'clock; that his paper " goes to bed " at twelve, and that if, in that short space, he can get on to paper some notion of the plot and the way in which the actors acquitted themselves he has done as much as can be reasonably expected. In my opinion the critic has done more in the circumstances than reason can demand; he has done marvels. Of all forms of imbecility that of the theatrical manager is the most absolute and the most abject. The merest glimmer of sanity would suggest that dramatic critics should attend the dress rehearsal, which should be made, as in France, a formal affair. (The editors of the popular press to be put upon what remains of their honour not to print any line concerning the production until the morning after the first performance; a short Bill to be passed by Parliament ensuring the decapitation of him who should steal a march upon his fellows.) The virtuosity with which the critic, writing for the next morning's paper, performs his almost impossible task is to me amazing. I must suppose the bustle of the stage to affect him in the same way in which the rattle of sticks in a dealer's yard affects your horse of mettle. Up go his head and tail. Away goes his screed whinneying and neighing, threatening to get out of hand if the nagsman have not a care. One claims for the heat of the playhouse that it operates in the brain like sherris-sack in the system of Falstaff. Another of our great critics has stated publicly that he has no views upon any play until a drive along the Embankment shall have refreshed his brain. Ensconced in his library and pressing against his heated brow cool volumes of Brunetière or of Croce, he gives the world the ultimate crystals of vexed thought. Unlike Mr. Walkley, I have no power of recovery the same evening. For my part, I must sleep off a play before I can form an opinion of its quality. Whenever, in that desperate *corps à corps* for hat and coat, my colleagues throw me a breathless " What do you think of the show ? " I reply, gasping, that as yet I do not know what I think of it. Inwardly I pray that, should I emerge from the cloakroom's bottle-neck alive, illumination may descend upon me on the morrow. Not for your Hotspur of criticism this luxury of suspended judgment! On his knee as the play progresses or, between the acts, in some furtive corner of the *foyer*, you will find him summing up, unfairly and not even squarely, and obviously only so far as the stage reached by the incompleted evidence.

In distant Aberdeen they go to press at eleven. Now there was once a certain crotchety Norwegian playwright who made one of his characters, dead before the play started, walk into a mill-race. Plain suicide, though perhaps of a not very intelligible order. Doubt-

16

Voluntary

less by ten o'clock on the first night of the first English
performance our synchronist had achieved a readable
lucidity in the darkness, actual and metaphorical. He
knew what he thought about the play. And then, at
half-past ten, our unaccountable playwright dropped his
third-act curtain on the declaration that if ever woman
was taken by the shoulders and resolutely immersed,
head held under till she drowned, Beata was that woman.
Too late ! In Aberdeen, next morning, the play must
treat of *felo-de-se.* Those leisurely gentlemen who write
for the London dailies may thank their stars for a kinder
fortune; they have a whole hour for readjustments.
But even they must be glad that, on the English stage,
the crop of plays like *Rosmersholm* is a thin one.

That articles written at lightning speed, combining
quick-firing with precision, should be accomplished at
all is to me a constant wonder. It is obvious that their
reproduction in book form can only be at the cost of
immensities of " scrutiny and titivation." But your
writer for a weekly review undergoes none of these
tortures. It is rare indeed that he has less than the
greater part of a week in which to deliver his soul, and
for fifteen hundred words that should suffice. The
writer who would take more will not grow rich by letters,
whilst he who wilfully takes less is a scamp. That
Frenchman, boasting of search for the proper word
through many weary weeks, we know now to have been
an unready, indolent fellow who lay on a sofa smoking
cigarettes, and mistook the weariness of gestation for the
pangs of labour. When the word is ready to be born,
it will be born, and not before. Nevertheless there is as
little excuse for slipshod workmanship, when a reason-

17

able measure of time is allowed, as there is for writing
with less than beautiful intention about an art having
to do with beauty.

Here we come upon the whole gift and crux of the
matter—the necessity for him who would write of the
theatre to compel beauty. Work from which beauty is
absent will not live, and the critic who has not one eye on
posterity is blind in both. Let me not be misunderstood.
I do not claim for this volume of essays that, a hundred
years hence, it will be found reposing in Streatham's
bow-window, next to the aspidistra, crosswise upon *If
Winter Comes*. I know the fate of my book. I realize
that, not a century, but a year hence, it will exist
only on some topmost shelf of the British Museum.
Yet this knowledge has not prevented me from putting
into each and every essay the utmost urgency and thrust
for beauty of which I am capable. The deed and not
the attempt confounds me. The function for which the
dramatic critic requires both his eyes is two-fold—his
present duty toward readers desiring to know which
theatres to visit and which to avoid, and his obligation to
the actor whom he, the critic, can alone preserve for
posterity. I will not labour the latter point; it is
become a commonplace. That upon which I would
insist is that the handing down of the actor can be done
only by the enlistment of beauty. Bensley, who
" looked, spoke, and moved like an old Castilian,"
Elliston, " joyousest of once embodied spirits," Jack
Palmer and Dicky Suett, Bannister, Munden, and Dodd
—all these come down to us not on account of the just-
ness of Lamb's estimate, but because of the beauty with
which he informed that estimate. Our knowledge of

Voluntary

Kean and Kemble comes to us through Hazlitt who, for all we can swear to the contrary, may have been mistaken as to these actors' graces and parts. Yet that excess, if it were excess, of appreciation is clothed in a prose of which the sinews and the suppleness delight us still; we read and re-read, not because of these dead mummers who can never be anything to us, but because of what they were to their memorialist. Of later critics I read W. T. Arnold for his sense of the theatre, Arthur Symons for his twilight beauty, Shaw for the racing engines of his powerful mind, Montague for his wit, Walkley for his urbanity, and Max for at least three of these reasons. The actors enshrined in the pages of these writers live because their remembrancers live; and they in turn live because they took beauty for their " line."

Some little time ago I discovered, amongst the litter of a second-hand bookshop, a scrap-album containing accounts cut out of the "Daily Telegraph" of all Irving's first nights at the Lyceum. Awed still as in the past of thirty years by the uncanny solicitations of that old man's genius, passionately though I worship in this, its decadence, the art of his great partner, I find these accounts unendurable. " Clement Scott," in huge letters, sprawls across their lack of style. It is a grave thought that if these players thus pitifully depicted had lived before my time I should have been able to form no opinion of them. I know of no page in any writer to which I can point and say: " Yes, that was Irving! " I know where to find passages which sum up Coquelin: " . . . the long upper lip that at will would let down like a drop curtain or curl back over the teeth in every width of

Voluntary

smile or grin from Tartuffe's to a yokel's, the tilted, sensitive nose—it seemed to flick like a terrier's." Or I can, at will, summon up a vision of Forbes-Robertson, whose Hamlet, " like a picture of Watts, could hang in a cathedral without seeming silly." But of Irving, of Ellen Terry, nothing. The modern critic does not take the trouble to record what the actor looks like. He takes it for granted that since the reader can visit the theatre for himself he can also decide for himself in what respects, say Mr. Arthur Bourchier looked his part admirably, or a shade less than admirably. But what about his reader's children, or children's children? Let us suppose that your old writer had been tucked away, as I was tucked away, at the last play—*The Risk*—in which I saw, or almost saw, that genial player. Debarred from any too particular account of that which he had hardly glimpsed, would not the old-fashioned critic have supplied the deficiency out of anterior knowledge? Since an ounce of practice is worth a pound of precept let me set down what I thought of Mr. Bourchier on this occasion. It happens that the dress circle at the Strand Theatre is shaped like certain brackets one used to connect with algebra. At about the fourth seat from the boxes there is a recess in the curve, and in that luckless coign was I ensconced. Nothing could I see of the stage, which was entirely cut off by the shoulder of my neighbour leaning forward. Craning my neck I could glimpse the right half of a room, but alas! that half held not Mr. Bourchier. During the greater part of his opening scene at the consulting table he was, therefore, to me completely invisible. An eclipse of the sun, even though partial,

20

Voluntary

may be interesting, a total eclipse of Mr. Bourchier is less so; all I could do was to listen. I suppose there is not a tone in that voice with which I am not familiar. Admonitory or persuasive, fulminatory or merely rallying, it announces its possessor as being ranged, if a trifle gruffly, yet very definitely on the side of the angels. Cavernous and proceeding out of the unknown, this trumpeting, now suave, now sinister, affected me like that of the Giant Blunderbore in the pantomime: that is to say, I was not really afraid. This was to be a symphony, not in outlandish Fa or Ut, but in thorough-going British Fee Fo Fum. There would be a fuss and a hurly-burly, but the child which is in me as in every playgoer was not alarmed. Towards the end of the act I discovered that Mr. Bourchier's features were discernible after all, dimly reflected in a mirror on the opposite side of the stage. But here again I was the victim of the familiar. This actor, strive how he may, cannot now encompass the *macabre*. His eyes shoot sparks, he compresses his countenance into wrinkles that he would fain have us take for the sardonic—the result is Panurge, not Mephistopheles. Or say that he resembles a canvas by that which should have been a French painter and not an adjective—Goguenard. The truth of the matter is that this actor has sat too often at the feet of Mr. Ian Hay, and caught from that popular magician too much of his easy-going spell. For the later acts the management, with great courtesy, found me a stall; but then the mischief was done, or rather, it was not to do. I could not believe that any serpent lurked in the folds of that benevolent chin, or was to come hissing out of that jovial mouth. And as for the pretence that the actor

Voluntary

was a surgeon who carved up healthy patients to stave off bankruptcy—go to! Within the limits of this disbelief Mr. Bourchier seemed to me to act really well. His bedside manner, twin shadow to Sir George Alexander's desperate assumptions of the gallant, was superb; his death scene an admirable affair of those convulsions and sawings of the nether lip which we may suppose to attend an unknown poison. But their whole sum was not eloquent of dissolution as some actors make us conceive that phenomenon. The great actors die; Mr. Bourchier simulated death admirably.

Would not your great writer have brought off, with every conviction of magnificence, that which I have done so baldly and ineffectively ? Baldly and ineffectively, I pray the reader to believe, not because I have not thought elaboration and effectiveness worth while. I have thought them worth while and you behold the unworthy result. Yet not so unworthy; I had not reprinted else. I claim not that the result does justice to this amiable mountain, but that you would not mistake the view for that of some lesser hillock. I have endeavoured in these pages to add to some earlier paintings, and to put on record something of the look, the gestures, and the accents of a few of the players of the present day. If the likenesses fail, they fail; I shall have no excuses to offer, and will not plead slap-dash and over-haste. The plain truth is that I have sat over them for many careful hours, and cannot improve them. The business of a writer is not to offend his reader; and to suggest that with more care he had written better is nothing less than an insult, for which the assumption of modesty is a cloak at once too thin and too false. I

Voluntary

claim, then, for these little essays that they are a link in the preservation of the actor between the old-time method of portraiture and that combination of cinematograph and gramophone to which, apparently, we are henceforward to entrust his renown. Let those who seek a formula of disparagement, finding it unwarrantable that another should lamely attempt that which his predecessors have done supremely, search no longer. I make them a present of " *Aesopes Asse* who, in emulation of the dogge, layde his two fore-feete very jocondly upon his master's shoulders: but looke how many blandishments the prety dogge received, under one, so many bastinadoes were redoubled upon the poor Asse's backe."

The trumpet of modesty duly blown, let me say that I care not a rap for blandishment or bastinado. I write not for reviewers who, the sooner they shall have declared that I quote too much, will the sooner obtain from their second-hand bookseller half the published price of this book; nor for merchants who, the more they have of wealth, possess the less of wit; nor for mimes who, lacking any perception of values, would rather be lauded extravagantly by a fool than appreciated justly by a writer of sense. The average actor, cocking his eye at the capacity of the trowel and despising the hand that holds it, considers nothing but the volume of his commendation, to the quality whereof he is supremely indifferent. How else can we explain his unvarying failure to include in his memoirs the best of his praise. Finer things have been said of the art of Mrs. Patrick Campbell than any she records in her ponderous volume. Of what critical use to her can it be to record that " We saw the slow development of the unescapable tragedy enveloping all the charaƈters as it were with vague and shadowy nets, and the light was one which never was on sea or land, and we were—speƈtators and aƈtors alike— such ſtuff as dreams are made of. . . . As one watches this Mélisande the words rise to one's lips, ' Will no one tell me what she sings ? ' For she, too, has caught the secret of ' old unhappy far-off things and battles long ago ' " ? Does not Mrs. Campbell realize that this bundle of *clichés* contains nothing which is not equally applicable to Sarah Bernhardt's Pelléas ? She does better to reproduce Mr. Walkley's " femme serpent," and John Davidson's " Paula is like an opal of many hues and luſtres, with ſtains of life, and wounds of passion through which the disaſtrous fires glow that shatter it in the end." Even here there is nothing that might not be said equally well of Everywoman. Emotional importunacy is Mrs. Campbell's " note," finely sounded in some provincial criticisms which she carefully ignores. Will artiſts never realize that criticism, like the commoneſt vat, ſtands on its own bottom, and that its value is not to be appraised in terms of the writer's initials ? Perhaps one ought to be thankful that aƈtors have not literary perception, that they are, from the writer's point of view, so supremely unintelligent. They would be less good aƈtors else.

This book is written, then, neither for the natural aƈtor who makes up in temperament for what he lacks in sense, nor for the intelleƈtual mime whose art is like a well-laid altar upon which the fire has not descended. For whom, then, is it written ? The answer is simple. It is written, firſt of all, for myself. Next, for all artiſts

Voluntary

appreciative of the difficulty as of the joy of craftsmanship, for all who after a mountain of labour have brought
forth so great a thing as a mouse. Then, for the inar-
ticulate, for those who, with swelling bosom, have lacked
the trick of speech. In the laſt resort I address myself
to the actor—presuming that he exiſt—who realizes
that complicated art, and not simple adulation, muſt be
the corner-ſtone of his praise. I do not say that the
appreciation of a Lear or a Hedda Gabler needs as
much skill as does their presentment; I say that both
creation and evaluation muſt have the quality of art.
Criticism is the actor's heightened and delighted perception reproduced in terms of the written word. No
actor will pretend to fathom Lear by the hoariness of his
locks; no actress to account for Hedda by ſtuffing her
bosom with pillows. Criticism of Lear will not be
satisfied with the ſtatement that never before wore he so
long a beard; of Hedda with a transcription of those
flatteries upon which our actresses love to batten—
" Hedda darling, you were wonderful to-night, *wonderful*, WONDERFUL."

A voluntary, my dictionary tells me, is " a piece
played by a musician, often extemporarily, according
to his fancy." I have preferred this word above
" preface " or " introduction," because under its cover
I may with more propriety indulge my fancy in the way
of a note or so of personal matters. My father was a
mine of information about the old actors of the 'sixties;
he talked to me at such length of Phelps and Fechter,
Charles Mathews, Alfred Wigan, and little Robson that
I came to know them as though I had seen them in the

Voluntary

flesh. From early years I fixed my gaze steadfastly upon
dramatic criticism. The " Manchester Guardian "
seemed a possible goal; the "Saturday Review" for ever
beyond reach. Yet I would try! I think it was Samuel
Smiles who, at about this period, pointed out to me that
there is nothing in this world which you cannot get if
you try hard enough. (The American Presidency was
his most cherished instance; as if anybody ever wanted
that!) In those days Prime Minister, King, or even
Pope was as nobody in comparison with him who
should be dramatic critic to the " Saturday Review."
I hold the same opinion still. The editorship attracted
me not, my ambition being temporal, not spiritual. St.
Paul, cheerfully confessing himself a fool, was not afraid
to laud his calling. Let me, a miserable critic, make
the proud boast: *Magnificabo apostolatum meum.*

And this brings me to two trifling grievances, trifling
yet real. I am tired of being twitted for my " obeis-
ances at the shrines " of X and Y and Z. I would not,
if I could, win fame at the coat-tails of another writer,
how famous soever; preferring to squat at the door
of the temple on my own hunkers. Cousinage is not
dependence. Then there is that little matter of quota-
tion in which the foolish see no more than a desire to
parade one's reading. Whereas nothing seems to me
to smack more of conceit than the deliberate avoidance of
the perfect expression simply because it was first found
by another. To foist upon the reader less good words
for the same idea simply because they happen to be one's
own is, to my mind, the last of vanity. It was my good
hap once to discover a phrase which seemed to me
exactly to fit the art of Sir Herbert Tree—" lavish

26

voicelessness." Frankly, I should deem the next writer
a fool who, squeamish in the matter of a loan, impoverished his page. He has no business to withhold from his
readers so lucky a find. (I cannot be accused of too
much conceit in this matter, since of some half million
words expended upon the theatre store is set upon
a paltry couple.) As for my own borrowings, I will be
equally frank: I am as unblushing a thief as many a
better man. Let my neighbour in the stalls drop me
some witty allusion and it shall go hard if I make no
place for it. I take my good where not only I but
others find it. Originality is the thief of time. To
resent the skilful use of another's wording betrays a
singular meanness in the reader; it is as though,
having paid a penny for the writer's thoughts, he should
object that his hireling has defrauded him of some part
of his labour. Montaigne has said the last word about
filching authors who, "amidst their trivial composi-
tions, intermingle and wrest in whole sentences taken
from ancient authors, supposing by such filching-theft
to purchase honour and reputation to themselves, doe
cleane contrarie. For this infinite varietie and dis-
semblance of lustres makes a face so wan, so il-favored,
and so uglie, in respect of theirs, that they lose much
more than gaine thereby." Yet no writer ever quoted
more; at a moderate estimate we may put Montaigne's
borrowings at one-tenth of his total matter. Bacon, in
his Essays, was not ashamed to make one hundred and
thirty-one quotations from the Latin alone! Strip from
this writer the fat of other men's minds, and it is
astonishing how little lean remains. To mitigate the
displeasure of those who dislike exotic growths I have

Voluntary

weeded my little garden carefully, collecting in my refuse-basket I know not how much weight of authority, but that which, in length, measures four yards and three inches exactly. In *Mary Queen of Drinkwater* I have quoted two passages of considerable length from Professor Rait's admirable monograph on Mary Stuart. This for the simple reason that, in my opinion, they embody facts or statements of alleged fact which should be known to anybody desirous of forming an opinion on the historical justice of this play. Let those of my reviewers who were familiar with these passages before they saw them in my pages cast their little pebbles. They won't hurt. I have also given the Professor's alternative estimates of Mary's character. They cannot be bettered, and I have no time to waste in the attempt.

" Prefaces, and passages, and excusations, and other speeches of reference to the person . . . though they seem to proceed of modesty, they are bravery." Thus Bacon, but not therefore the gospel.

Marie Lloyd

WHEN, IN THE TOTTENHAM COURT Road, I saw, tucked under the newsboy's arm, the sheet which announced that Marie Lloyd was dead, everything around me became still. The street lost its hubbub, and for a space I was alone with a personal sorrow. In moments of emotion one is apt to notice the little things, and at once I remarked that, on the poster, the artist's name was prefaced with the word "Miss." Death, it seemed, laying his hand upon her who was known over the whole English-speaking world as "Marie," must use more ceremony. "Marie"—pronounced with the broad vowel beloved of the Cockney—was in everybody's mouth that day, in club and barrack-room, in bar-parlour and in modest home. On the high seas "Marie's dead" would be droned from ship to ship. Returning from Kempton a party of bookmakers fell to speaking of the dead artist. One said, with tears in his eyes, "She had a heart, had Marie!" "The size of Waterloo Station," another rejoined. Her abounding generosity was a commonplace of the profession. She would go down to Hoxton, where she was born, and make lavish distribution to the street-urchins of boots and shoes which she fitted with her own hands. She had numberless pensioners dependent upon her charity. She earned some two hundred thousand pounds, and gave it all away. "God rest her," said the bookmaker who had

Marie Lloyd

firſt spoken, and bared his head. That night, at Black-friars Ring, a bruiser with the marks of many fights declared: " We shan't none of us see the likes o' Marie again. She was a great artiſt." Those who know that soundness must underlie a boxer's brilliance before he receives the title of " artiſt," will recognize the force of this tribute. If the music-hall singer, embodying a social ſtratum to those who know it like their hand, had deviated from truth by so much as a finger's breadth, she would not have received this higheſt meed of praise. To those whose verdiƈt is based upon the moſt positive of evidence such fancy things as implications are without meaning. Faƈts are faƈts, alike in the New Cut or in Leicester Square. Marie Lloyd's charaƈters knew no parishes but these; they were born in one and rose to the other. " Sank," the moraliſt will exclaim, true to his eternal preoccupation, and for ever beside the point. Morality is a philosophy of life; this realiſt presented types of human charaƈter and drew no moral.

It was not, however, from a world of bullies or the lower deck that Marie Lloyd drew her chief support. She was enormously popular with the class which lives in villas and makes a fetish of respeƈtability. To placate these, would-be apologiſts have pleaded that " whilſt many of the songs were in themselves offensive, the manner of their delivery took away the offence." This is the pureſt nonsense. The genius of this *diseuse* consiſted in the skill and emphasis with which she drove home the " offensive " point. She employed a whole armoury of shrugs and leers, and to reveal every cranny of the mind utilized each articulation of the body. Frank in geſture as Fielding was in phrase, her page of

Marie Lloyd

life was as outspoken and as sure. Hottentot and
Eskimo knowing no English, the respectable burgess
priding himself on his ignorance of the way of the
saloon-lounge, would yet recognize from the artist's
pantomime the burden of her song. She gave you the
frankly raffish wink which the courtesan tips to her
gigolo, together with the hard stare of the streets; and thus
made you free of an old profession. " No one was ever
the worse for her performance." Everything depends,
surely, upon what these squeamish critics mean by
" offensive " and " worse." It will not be claimed, I
think, that " A Little of What you Fancy Does you
Good " turned the young men out of the heated music-
hall into the Strand determined to look neither to the
right nor to the left. Marie Lloyd sang, as Rabelais
wrote, for good Pantagruelists and no others, and
chastity had to look elsewhere for a minister.

" Inside the Horsel here the air is hot,
Right little peace one hath for it, God wot,"

was the last reflection conveyed from that Hill of Venus
which was the stage of the Tivoli Music Hall. Hoxton's
daughter was as much the embodiment of her period as
some more pretentious folk. She reduced to the comprehension of butcher's-boy and clerk those limbs
moving " as melodies yet " to quite unpardonable
music, all that meaningless tosh about " curing the soul
by means of the senses." Little patience, we may be
sure, had the comédienne with the original form of
these nostrums for sick minds. She translated them
into tonics for the healthy body; she preached the world
and the flesh, and gloried in their being the very devil.

31

Marie Lloyd

None ever left the theatre feeling " better " for her songs. From that blight, at least, they were free. That which she sang was an old hymn which, on the music-hall stage, will not be repeated. *Explicit Laus Veneris.*

From any cold-blooded, reasoned immorality her songs were entirely free. Flaubert, you remember, makes one of his characters conjure up the red lamp of a brothel with the reflection that of all life's experiences this youthful one was the most truly happy. Marie Lloyd's honest spirit would have utterly disdained so pitiful a philosophy. The sailor of whom she sang might, as the result of an encounter in Piccadilly, miss his ship, but a mere incident would not turn him, like Flaubert's sentimental fellow, eternally adrift. There was no decadent Latin taint about Marie; she was almost saltily British. Villadom accepted her in the way it accepts the gay dog who makes no secret of his gaiety. Villadom will have nothing to do with the sad fellow whose pleasure is furtive, and it recognized that there was nothing sad or secret about its idol. Marie knew that the great English public will open its arms to vice, provided it is presented as a frolic. She knew, though she could not have put her knowledge into words, that her art was one with the tradition of English letters, which has always envisaged the seamy side of life with gusto rather than with deprecation. Yvette Guilbert harrowed the soul with the pathos of her street-walkers; Marie Lloyd had intense delight in her draggle-tails. She showed them in their splendour, not in their misery; the mopishness and squalor of their end were not for her. And that is why, when she came to the portrayal of elderly baggages, she refrained from

Marie Lloyd

showing them as pendants to her courtesans. A French artist would have insisted upon the inevitable descent to the procuress, whereas the English artist rejected even Mother Peachum. Instead she gave happy life to battered harridans ludicrous in the sight of man, if not of God; diving into their very entrails for the unstilled riot which made old Jenny steal from her husband's bed to dance at the ball. Again she proved herself an infinitely greater realist than others more highly esteemed. She depicted the delight of humble life, the infinite joy of mean streets. When some jovial crone, emerging from the wings, flung at an unseen, routed foe a Parthian " And it wouldn't take me long, neither! " you settled in your stall to listen to a reading from the Book of Low Life. There was unction here, and a smack of the lips over a Vulgate the accuracy of which, divined by the boxes, was eagerly checked by the gallery. Was Marie Lloyd vulgar ? Undoubtedly. That jovial quality was her darling glory. She relished and expounded those things which she knew to be dear to the common heart.

Marie had the *petite frimousse éveillée*, the wideawake little " mug " which Sarcey noted in Réjane. Her " dial," as the Cockney would put it, was the most expressive on the halls. She had beautiful hands and feet. She knew every board on the stage and every inch of every board, and in the perfection of her technical accomplishment rivalled her great contemporary of another world, Mrs. Kendal. Briefly, she knew her business. But it is not my purpose to talk now of technical excellence. Rather would I dwell on the fact that she was adored by the lowest classes, by the

Marie Lloyd

middle people, and by the swells. " I hope," she said in a little speech before the curtain at her last appearance at the Alhambra, " I hope I may, *without bigotry*, allude to my past triumphs." Poor soul, it is we who should ask to be delivered from that vice. Marie broadened life and showed it, not as a mean affair of refusal and restraint, but as a boon to be lustily enjoyed. She redeemed us from virtue too strait-laced, and her great heart cracked too soon.

Three Plays of Ibsen

The Pretenders. O.U.D.S.
Hedda Gabler. Everyman Theatre.
John Gabriel Borkman. Everyman Theatre.

IBSEN'S *THE PRETENDERS* IS HIS sternest, grimmest glorification of that hard condition, twin-born with greatness, which has irked so many self-centred rulers to no more than a gentle melancholy. The English Henry's "What infinite heart's-ease must kings neglect, that private men enjoy!" is a purely selfish lament. "Every one must go who is too dear to the King!" cries Haakon, banishing in a single self-immolatory swoop both his mother and his mistress. Here, in a nutshell, is the philosophy of kingship. Kings are to consider not how jolly a thing it is "to sit three steps above the floor," but how best they may fulfil their trustee-ship and serve the kinghood which is in their meanest subjects. Ibsen blares this nineteenth-century thought through a thirteenth-century trumpet. Harald the Fairhaired conceived it better for King Harald that Norway should have one ruler in place of a hundred. Haakon sees that it is better for Norway that she should be a "nation" instead of a "kingdom." It is the people who exist by divine right and not their kings. Ibsen makes immense play with the idea that a country which is only a kingdom is "a church which has not been consecrated."

Three Plays of Ibsen

Earl Skule, who would have Haakon's place, owes his defeat to his failure to rise to the heights of the " great kingly thought " which he would usurp. His son, believing in the authenticity of Skule's thought, breaks open the church and violates the shrine that his father may be crowned king. This misfeasance works the wrong way; the superstitious soldiery defect. Whereupon Skule, in all humility, gives up the ghost. " A man may die for the sake of the life-work of another; but if he is to live, he must live for his own." And Haakon, who can trample the pride of rule under foot, goes forward to unwilling personal victory. " His body blocks my path." *Dagfinn:* " If Haakon is to go forward, it must be over Skule's body! " *Haakon:* " In God's name, then! "

It is not to be imagined that this *leit-motif* is easily detached. Even at this early date Ibsen was busy at his baffling game of keeping two plots going, a ground-floor of bricks and mortar and a symbolical superstructure. Fail to get the hang of the upper storey and you may well think yourself in the basement of a lunatic asylum. Rosmer inviting Rebecca to throw herself into the mill-race " to show her confidence," Hedda handing Lövborg the pistol, Solness toppling off his steeple with Hilda crying " Bravo! "—people really don't do such things, and it takes all Ibsen's mature genius to persuade us that with an extra spiritual dimension this may be sanity. But at thirty-five he was not very clever at the game. The ground-floor of *The Pretenders,* with its story of changelings and intercepted letters, is as complicated as a play by Sardou or Scribe. It is also a great deal less lucid, with the result that in fumbling for the

36

symbolical staircase you bark your shins against a good
deal of downstairs mahogany. To make confusion
worse confounded add the overpowering figure of
Bishop Nicholas. In the early acts this character is all
the darkling imagination and inveterate horror of old-
fashioned melodrama. It is only at the end of his
tremendous death-scene that you in any way connect him
with the play's philosophical basis. Only at the very end
are you allowed to see that his malignancy springs from
innate disability to grasp that kind of power which
Haakon despises and Skule cannot leave behind. This
materially towering character pulls all the play's strings;
it is only at the last that you perceive him to have a
finger in the philosophic pie. All this makes the play
very difficult to act. There is hardly any "furniture"
in the later and avowedly symbolical dramas. Rosmer
has a hat and stick, Hilda Wangel a kit-bag, and so on,
but these are obvious imponderabilia. Whereas *The
Pretenders* makes enormous parade with trials by ordeal,
armies in rout, the paraphernalia of prelacy, and
panoplied death-beds such as actors love. The dying of
Bishop Nicholas is a collector's piece in the way of
virtuosity. Unfortunately it occurs in the middle of the
play, with the result that no great actor will look at it.
If only the bishop could have been kept going to the end,
we may be sure that old Irving would have had a shot
at him.

Ibsen, we are told, used the historical struggle
between Haakon and Skule to mirror his own unwilling
jealousy of his successful rival Björnson. We need not
labour this theory too much. It fits, but then these
things always do fit. Skule has the uneasy conscious-

37

ness that the other's triumph is at once easy and deserved. Haakon possesses, as Bishop Nicholas puts it, *ingenium*, or the quality which Lord Beaverbrook and Mr. Selfridge insist upon as the true foundation of success. Haakon is the favourite of fortune, the born leader, begetting thoughts greater than he understands, following a path of which he cannot see the end. Skule's jealousy does not prevent him from recognizing his rival's great merits; it is in fact he who is their chief exponent and, as jealous Ibsen's mouthpiece, does the bulk of the talking. In this great wilderness of a play much, perforce, must be cut, but it is a pity, surely, to cut the essential clues, as was done at the performance by the O.U.D.S. Obviously Haakon must have the "great kingly thought" before Skule can be jealous of it. Unfortunately his sacrifice of mother and mistress was cut and his reluctance from a personal victory minimized. Some of the critics, writing of the performance under their eyes, described Haakon as a man of physical courage only. This, it seems to me, is entirely to misunderstand the character. "Am I to think that the king is made of different stuff from me?" wails Skule. Of course he is; of different and better stuff. That's the whole point. Haakon is inclined to talk a bit tall, through his spiritual hat, as it were. Like all Ibsen's great men he is a bit of a braggart. His spiritual bragging cut, Mr. E. L. Bush (Trin.) could perhaps do no other than play him like some stalwart, boasting for the dedans in the Oxford tennis-court. This it probably was which misled the critics. Earl Skule was much nearer the Ibsen spirit. I do not know what Mr. A. H. Howland (Worc.) thought of the part, but he looked hot and bothered, which was exactly right. Mr. G. G. Edwards (Oriel) gave a finely modulated, subtle performance of the most grateful part ever devised for an actor, except, of course, for the deep damnation of its cutting off in the middle of the evening.

Hedda Gabler is a tremendous play in any but the strict sense of the word. It contains nothing of awe or terror, nothing to make us fearful lest our own *exaltées* should take to pistol-practice in the garden. Yet what a vogue was Hedda's in that heyday of long ago! Her lure was largely that of the incomprehensible. Who could read her? " *Kennen Sie Ibsen?* " " *Nein, wie macht man das?* " was a passing joke. But " How should Hedda be played? " persisted. Mr. Archer declared her to be the victim of hyperæsthesia; Mr. Beerbohm plumped for a woman under-sexed and under-vitalized. Mr. Shaw made some violently sensible, unforgettable pronouncement which I have forgotten; Mr. Grant Allen pretended that he was sent in to dinner with her every evening. All of which made one envious of that moral courage which could insist that the king in the fairy-story was without clothes. These clever persons seemed to me to be labelling something which was not there. Hedda, as she existed in real life before Ibsen's flaming genius transfigured her, was an earlier sister of the wood-carving young woman in " Kipps." She was lymphatic, and a nuisance to any normally constituted society. But she was not dangerous, as was the Hedda of the play.

Some women do some of the things which Ibsen's

heroine does, but no woman perpetrates them all. Let me admit that Hedda was bored, oh exquisitely bored, with Tesman, his slippers, his aunts, his aunts' illnesses and dyings and bonnets and midwifely pleasantries, Tesman's researches into the domestic industries of Brabant, his lack of talent, his spinelessness. Let me take into account the atmosphere of yesterday's cold mutton which pervades these provincials at heart, the insufferable tedium of even the capital in a country of stoves and goloshes. Let me remember that Hedda was " ninety-ish " in a society which saw not the modish possibilities. All this explains why she should marry— Tesman, in the worst event—philander with Brack, and ache to have a finger in the Lövborg pie. Fastidious yet curious, repelled by life yet attracted, she was the descendant of the patrician who, aloof from the arena, was sufficiently interested to turn down her thumb. Hedda has been called " mesquine." It is just that pinchbeck quality which leads her to steal Lövborg from Mrs. Elvsted, to provoke his befuddlement and to destroy his masterpiece. But that she would have put the pistol into his hand or used its fellow against herself I do not believe, nor will all the courtier-like worshippers of Ibsen make me believe. There is no symbolism in *Hedda Gabler* upon which we can ride off into the clouds. When Hilda Wangel claps her hands at Solness's fall and acclaims it as a magnificent achievement, we know that she is speaking a language to which common sense holds no key. But there is nothing undecipherable about the present play. Put to the touchstone of rationality, it leaves a doubtful streak. Hedda, conceivably, would have urged Lövborg to the precipice; she gives no sign of the courage needful for that ultimate push. Nor yet for her own desperate leap. Brack's " People don't do such things " is Ibsen's effort to prevent criticism, just as a playwright will sometimes strive to get behind verisimilitude by putting into the mouth of a character some such phrase as " If we were people in a play . . . "

·Not in the least like Ibsen's Hedda, Mrs. Patrick Campbell gives us a magnificent portrait of somebody else. Consider Ibsen's stage-directions and then look upon the actress's physical qualifications. Hedda's hair is of a " medium brown, not particularly abundant." Mrs. Campbell wears her black mane as it were a thunder-cloud. Hedda's eyes are " steel-grey, expressive of cold, unruffled repose." Mrs. Campbell's are twin-craters, presaging disaster. One actress, and one only, could be less Hedda, and that is Sarah. Duse got out of the necessity for interpretation by playing the part as ·though she were half-asleep, " a somnolent guardian-angel " someone called her. Mrs. Campbell's Hedda of the first act is curiously becalmed, her dead-white face the sail riding the sullen sea of existence and awaiting the gathering storm. A wave of petty provocation strikes her and she shivers as a boat will shiver. The actress loads the vessel with the utmost of tragic beauty. Ever, to change the metaphor, more the antique Roman than the Norsewoman of the cold gaze and impoverished chignon, Mrs. Campbell fills the eye which Ibsen left empty. She gives the old haunting quest for beauty, the imperious line, the importunate sweep of the throat. Once more we hear the liquid utterance, fluent yet staccato, the old, exquisite phrasing. With what cruel delight does she torture her commonplace, successful rival, silly Mrs. Elvsted! What abyss of egoism is opened beneath our feet when, to the fretting Tesman hasting to Aunt Rina's death-bed, she throws that mocking " Oh, if you run——! "

Yet I cannot help feeling that Mrs. Campbell's very magnificence makes nonsense of the play. She makes it impossible for us to believe that she would ever have married Tesman. " There is a world elsewhere " we feel she would have cried, turning her back upon Christiania. This is more Stella Gabler than Hedda, a creature whose bearing, outline, and colour suggest triumphant traipsing at the heels of fame. With her hand on extravagant hip, her mannered pose, her geranium-coloured shawl the actress recalled the canvases of Goya. Hedda, really, should look like one of Miss Jean Cadell's old maids startled out of her virginity. It is in the last act that Mrs. Campbell is nearest to Ibsen. Here she delivers her challenge to life as though she were turned into stone; the throat has lost its line of luxury, is marble now.

If Tesman is to be played along conventional lines it follows that he must hedge this Hedda in with a kind of twittering imbecility. It is difficult to get away from the conventional rendering, which is obviously what Ibsen intended.

" I don't see anything absolutely ridiculous about him. Do you? " says Hedda. And Brack replies, " Ridiculous ? N—no— I shouldn't exactly say so——."

This, in itself, is a confession, but one which, at Hampstead, is almost too heavily underlined.

Three Plays of Ibsen

The question has been asked, " What, exactly, are we supposed to learn from the educational drama ? Is it suggested that anyone goes to the theatre in order to obtain light on philosophy, economics, sociology, politics, eugenics ? " The question could not have been more happily framed. Yes, it is so suggested. The essential function of art, including that of the " educational " drama, is to give forth illumination. But thereby is not meant the bull's-eye of the policeman, the beacon of the coastguard, the X-ray of the consultant. These partake, in Bacon's phrase, of the " dry light " of the man of science. When the specialist turns a narrow beam into the cavern of your throat, he uses the torch in a way essentially non-artistic. When, sinking the case in the individual, he turns his apprehension upon you, suffusing it with emotion of his own, he becomes the artist, and the light he uses is the sacred lamp. Art has nothing to do with discovery, elucidation, or moral precept. Its function is simply to invigorate the imagination. The theatre is not a night-school. Its drama illumines philosophy, sociology, politics, and the rest by reflection, in that it lights up the philosopher, the sociologist, and the politician. The characters of the " non-educational " dramatist may exhibit wisdom, gumption or guile, but they will not be the peculiar discernment of the philosopher, the essential *nous* of the sociologist, the characteristic cheats of the politician. Equally becoming duke or commoner, his differentiations throw no light upon their wearers' walk of life. Whereas the " educational " dramatist, Shakespeare for example, delights in the essential quality of his characters. He brings men's talk home to their business and bosoms. Every inch of Lear is absorbed in kingship. Henry V is greateſt, not in his sentimental rhapsodies, but in his acceptance of responsibility. Falstaff, taking three pounds to free Mouldy and Bullcalf, throws a light on Elizabethan tribunals. Angelo is any chairman of Watch committees. There is hardly a figure in the plays which is not ablaze with philosophic, political, and social significance. But to call Shakespeare an " educational " dramatiſt is nonsense. There's no such thing. Dramatiſts are either good or bad. Shakespeare happens to be good.

Mark how another good dramatiſt, Ibsen, treats the theme of *John Gabriel Borkman,* and think how a less good dramatiſt would have treated it. Can we not see the excitement which the inferior playwright would have got out of this feuilleton of misappropriation and treachery, Borkman's sacrifice of one earneſt siſter and espousal of that gallsome other, his deteſtion, imprisonment, and downfall ? Ibsen raises the curtain exaſtly where the other would have dropped it. Five years have passed, the mansion's only traffic is the solitary pacing in the garret. The man is prisoner to his own soul. Not for a moment will Ibsen leave the miner in Borkman out of account. The great passage: " I love you, prisoned millions, as you lie there spell-bound in the deeps and the darkness! I love you, unborn treasures yearning for the light! I love you with all your shining train of power and glory! " gives significance to Borkman's firſt words: " I am a miner's son." He lends point to Stevenson's " I have heard the beſt kind of talk on technicalities from such rare and happy persons as both know and love their business." From the aſtual

Three Plays of Ibsen

misfortune of his mines and misappropriations, Borkman rises to the spiritual plane. "He had gone to ruin
with a kind of kingly *abandon*, like one who condes-
cended; but once ruined, with the lights all out, he
fought as for a kingdom." Something of this is the clue
to the play. Borkman was never nearer to life than in
the moment of his death. This maśterpiece, for it is a
maśterpiece, gives "exaćt information" about power
and the effećt of power on the human mind. It gives a
clearer apprehension of Ibsen himself, of Napoleon, of
Lord Northcliffe, of Jabez Balfour. It teaches more
philosophy than all your pragmatiśts put together. It is
the answer to the queśtion with which we began.

The play, in the theatre, is apt to be "difficult."
There is no positive virtue in dingy parlours hung with
penitential gloom. These things should be minimized
by the producer and not accentuated. Mr. Theodore
Komisarjevsky, at the Everyman Theatre, raised his
curtain on total night. Slowly we became aware
of something that might be firelight, chairs, tables,
human lineaments. It was all rather like the grave
giving up its dead. The aćtors spoke from another
world; their features were "composed." The tones of
Borkman came from the cellerage of his paśt. With his
sombrero, frock-coat, and śtout boots he was, to outward
showing, subśtantial. But with his grey beard and
glittering eye, he was a man "all light, a seraph-man,"
śtanding on his own corse. Mr. Dyall was intellećtually
magnificent, and Mr. Dodd brought tears. The ladies
were overweighted. I should like to suggeśt that Mrs.
Wilton's insiśtence upon Erhart's goloshes be omitted.
There is something peculiarly repugnant about "go-

45

loshes." All Manchester is in that word. Then the whole play should be taken much faster, allowing us no time to reflect that people do not enter upon heart-to-heart talks after years of absence and a journey in Norwegian mid-winter without at least a dish of tea, or propose to spend the rest of their lives upon snowbound plateaux unprovided with the smallest suit-case. Ibsen should be played with less obsequiousness, just as though he were an ordinary playwright writing for the ordinary theatre. Which, of course, he was.

Hail Punch, and Farewell!

Five Plays. The Little Theatre

I F YOU WERE TO COMPARE THE type of character portrayed in a normal melodrama and at the Grand Guignol, you would probably declare for the former as approximating more nearly to the life-like, the latter to the phantasmal. You would be wrong. In the new series at the Little Theatre the humanity is entirely credible; in a melodrama such as that now being performed at the Duke of York's it is strictly lunatic.

Or, perhaps, not strictly. For my dictionary gives: LUNATIC, *n.*, a madman; a person of unsound mind; an insane person, *esp.* one who has lucid intervals. But none of the people in *The Night Cap* has lucid intervals. Mad, without qualification, must be the bank-director who holds it immoral to rob his depositors and moral to recoup them at the expense of his insurance company. Imbecile the hero who marries his ward at midnight, before committing suicide, because she happens to have slept under his roof. Witless beyond redemption the young woman who, assured that " this is not to be an actual marriage," murmurs " Reely ? " and, burying her face in her so-called lover's breast, is no more curious. Cretinous the financier who holds incitement to murder more honourable than bankruptcy. Faced with this endemic idiocy, I did not wonder at a little

47

Hail Punch, and Farewell!

excitable old Jewish lady who, as the curtain fell on the first act, exclaimed: "Am I *meschügge*, or are these people?" Her difficulty was to understand a society in which the rational did not apply. In a world in which gravitation has ceased to act, people, one understands, walk the ceiling as conveniently as the floor. So, in this play, there is no groundwork of normality upon which to found the abnormal. Is it a question of murder or suicide, then is conscience plated with triple rhinoceros. Is it a question of female delicacy, then that conscience reels at a breath of thistledown. The play is dull, dull, dull as its reiterated pistol-shots. For to startle you must have some background of the expected; to amuse, some implication of the serious. There is a well-known music-hall "absurdity" at the end of which Mr. Ernie Lotinga shoots hero and heroine, villain, accomplice, and police. Of this order is this play. In its peculiar idiom the audience are just "boobs." The authors are "stringing" them, and they are "falling for it." You might have taken it all for spoof had it not been for Mr. Loraine, non-committal, humourless, four-square as a policeman on point-duty. He arranged his fraud, marriage, affairs, and quietus in level grating monotone, with the occasional perfunctory pause before a word which, in the Adelphi scale, indicates emotion. It was as though the actor, not knowing what to make of the play, had wilfully abrogated his intelligence. Like a billiard-player playing for safety, Mr. Loraine left every sentence which might convey meaning under the cushion. Mr. Spencer Trevor, as the director-dervish executing a dance of comic perturbation around and upon the body of his dead colleague, clowned it very

48

Hail Punch, and Farewell!

cleverly. But it was the play which roused my little old lady to a final expostulation: "What a wonderful people are the English! Nothing do they throw. No benches do they break. *Das Theater steht noch da!*"

The chief interest of the plays at the Little Theatre lies in the opposition of normal humanity and abnormal circumstance. Go raking in an ant-heap and the little creatures, though perturbed, will retain their ant-like senses in the face of obtrusion. The essence of Grand Guignolism is that however inexplicable, however ghostly the interference, man shall retain his dignity. Sane he shuns the asylum, in health the charnel-house. It is abnormal for a good woman to destroy a man out of compassion, for a toy-soldier to give his wooden life, for a regiment to be inoculated with rabies. Yet you never felt that you were not in contact with real people. Credit for this must be given in large measure to the extraordinary finish of the actors. From the little news-vendor who whips out his paper as though he were born to the kerb, palm uppermost and sheet curtaining the fingers, to Mr. Bealby's eternal barman, a figure of love and gusto, from the child in the cot to Miss Thorndike's uttermost transmogrification, there was not an accent or a gesture which was not related to humanity. Perhaps this was the least true of the first piece. I was unfortunately placed so as to suffer an extraordinary tide of late-comers. About every seventh wave I caught a glimpse of Mr. Bealby in a sea of troubles, baffled by cliffs too beetling to be practicable. High and dry, Miss Thorndike could be heard flintily interjecting: "Oh Bob!" Unpossessed of anything in the nature of a life-line, she preferred to fend him off with a

49

Hail Punch, and Farewell!

long pole, finally keeping the wretch under till he was drowned. The part is hardly worthy of Miss Thorndike, and it would be gracious and politic of her to leave it to some beginner. Politic because it would do away with one of her sets of crying. Her extraordinary whimper, like that of a small horse, is both unconventional and effective, but twice in one evening is enough.

With the company's fidelity to one side of truth goes a curious indifference to that other facet which is beauty. Mr. Levy has not recruited a single fine voice. Mr. Bealby has an organ of immense power, but it is as though some forest-giant were being sawn into a thousand coffin-planks. Mr. Russell Thorndike's lugubrious snarl—the accents of George Formby turned First Witch—weary a little and are not always suitable. This raven croaks itself hoarse upon too many battlements. Any art which dabbles in the unbeautiful must have exquisite compensation, and that is why Beardsley for his most revolting curve used his most entrancing line. On the stage delicate modulation brings increase of horror. French actors know this and transform the croaking sinister into some unearthly carillon. The company at the Little Theatre is good enough to make us desire such music. Both Mr. Bealby and Mr. Thorndike were excellent in the play about hydrophobia. So was Mr. George Owen. So was Mr. Casson. So was everybody. The play arouses some nice questions about the function of horror as distinct from terror. If it be permissible to exhibit one victim in the throes, must we boggle at fifteen hundred ? Would five hundred be reasonable ? Or fifty a lawful compromise ? Mr.

Hail Punch, and Farewell!

Stanley Logan's *De Mortuis*, in which a funeral party
discusses, over refreshment, the murder of a *souteneur*,
is like a plate from Hogarth. It makes no concessions to
sentiment. A poor girl, in accepting an honest mate,
had no further earnings to give the bully who was her
brother. He, taunting the lover, was struck down.
The gin-sodden mother who should, by all the canons of
squeamishness, admit forgiveness to her obsequious riot,
strips every rag from her shameful daughter. All this is
debated, interminably. Also it is set some distance away
from us, as in a frame. For behind the bar, aloof,
detached, indifferent to human rabble as was ever
Hogarthian monkey, yet presidential by virtue of his
office, looms the immortal host. Manipulated by Mr.
Bealby, the handles of the beer-engine are primal as
original boughs. Conning unmoved philosophies
beneath his blond and plastered thatch, the sage creature
who, like ourselves, is also a spectator, dispenses not
poppy, not mandragora, but the tots which bring for-
getfulness to his brethren who walk erect.

Delight is the ultimate reason and justification for the
theatre, as for all art, and it is mere aesthetic snobbery
to pretend that five hours of *Hamlet* badly played are
more pleasurable than five half-hours of lesser import
eked out with magnificent acting. One forgives the
moderate level of accomplishment at the " Old Vic " in
virtue of the cause, just as the innocuous bleating of
Vincent Wallace's sheepish melodies may be conceived
as being more tuneful than the cries of the hucksters at
the stalls without. It is a legacy of Puritan thought
which inclines one to overlook deficiency in execution on

the score of moral intention. But there should be give and take, even in Puritanism. Shall not brilliance of achievement cover up a trifle of outspokenness ? Not one of the plays at the Little Theatre has seemed to me open to intelligent objection. There is a function in sheer horror which Aristotle, obsessed by his theory of pity and terror, stupidly failed to recognize. The streaming sockets of Œdipus, the severed head of Barnardine, the butchery by Evadne of the king among his pillows, belong as definitely to horror as the exploits of Professor Plume or the old women in the mad-house. (Modern critics get over the frightful spectacle of a Mounet-Sully with blood gushing from those two black holes in the head of Œdipus by quibbling over the word " horror.") It is the *imminence* of the horrible which is the essence of Grand Guignol. To compare those happenings upon which the curtain falls in the dead nick of time, or, at worst, upon the heel of accomplishment, with the drawn-out spectacle of a horse disembowelled in the bull-ring is to lack the right kind of sensitiveness. As for the rawer comedies, it is to be maintained that a deeper vulgarity and a subtler demoralization of thought and feeling underlie a single average play produced at our properer theatres than in all the Grand Guignol frisks put together. It were wiser to expose a child to the worst excesses of the Little Theatre than to the debasing commonness of the average " wholesome " play. The stage is an impartial mirror, reflective of the ignoble as of the noble. These crude comedies make a mock of the tawdry; the sentimental theatre enhances it.

Above all, Mr. Levy has given us a producer who is not an upholsterer. Mr. Lewis Casson can be trusted

Hail Punch, and Farewell!

to put his money into the brains of his artists and not into the legs of his chairs. He gives us the only kind of scenery which your true lover of acting cares anything at all about; and that is none. His settings are no more than a suggestion of the frame in which the thing portrayed might be supposed to happen. You think of the frame, if you think of it at all, as of a good illustration in a book, a " remembrancer " of the text. Of all the splendours inflicted on me in forty theatres during the last twelve months, I remember but two—a brown sail jutting up over London Bridge in the " Old Vic " production of *Wat Tyler* and one or two of Mr. Casson's lightings, instinct with foreboding and disaster.

To produce, says Johnson's Dictionary, means to generate. Mr. Casson brings forth life; others stifle it with their expensive swaddling clouts. One or two artists there have been in the company into whom not even the Arch-Producer has breathed the breath of stage-existence. With these, of course, Mr. Casson has been able to do nothing. But what has he not done with the others ? It is not sufficiently recognized how good an actor Mr. Casson is. He has not, Heaven be praised, the meaningless accent, pointless gesture, and insignificant grimace of your West End walking-gentleman. Rightly he abhors the weak and the washy; sometimes even in his characters you trace the corroding influence of a mind too strong. In the presence of the sinister he keeps the spectator's hold on sanity. You would think, perhaps, that this actor could not attain to fun. Yet, by sheer intellectual grit, he can bring forth an imitation of the comic. Meredith, driving the point home about comedy, might have been inspired by this actor. I

Hail Punch, and Farewell!

admire his present attainments and those of his leading lady all the more in that I remember the days when they were both—oh, so very much less good. Miss Thorndike was once frost and snow, never, you would have said from her Mrs. Barthwick, to be thawed to any kind of humanity. She is not quite human even now. Peevishness has grown to tragic size, yet still the actress alternates between a rehearsed and mechanical gibber and an unnatural calm. She has pathos, feeling for beauty, and a very rare quality of moral dignity. Her mere presence in a play is astringent and antiseptic, so that the fragments of parts which she has played during the past two years seem to me to be no more than studies for some vast, irreproachable cartoon. What she now needs is a dramatist to stand up to her. The passing of Punch is a serious blow to the lighter side of English drama. Hail, old friend, and farewell!

A Lance for Jane

Jane Clegg, by St. John Ervine.   New Theatre.

"KOMMT ZEIT, KOMMT RATH," says the old proverb.   The morning after the *première* at the New Theatre or, more accurately, its newspapers, brought me not reflection, but perplexity and doubt.   I knew what I thought of the previous evening's experience, which had been soul-stirring and fraught with consequence; the perplexity and doubt concerned some other people.   For obvious reasons I never read criticisms of plays till my own work is done.   Yet that morning I felt that I could not refrain.   The night before had seemed to me to mark a great occasion in the English theatre, one comparable with the first " commercial " productions of Ibsen and Shaw, the advent of the Irish Players, the establishment of Repertory Theatres in our big cities.   For had not our most responsible actress deliberately challenged fortune, not with some splurgy rubbish, Sardou or another, but with a play as English as the " ordinary " of the commercial traveller, a masterpiece small in scope but of perfect craftsmanship and truth, a slice torn out of the heart of things, in which her part was the least showy ?   Had not the house resounded with a quality of applause from which the spurious first-night ring was entirely absent ?   Had it not wept ?   Had I not

A Lance for Jane

left the theatre treading upon air, resolved to tear to bits
—*anglice*, reserve for another occasion—that subtle
analysis of the art of a great actress over which I had
spent the previous week-end? Fine writing on fine
occasions is an impertinence. Besides, it isn't any good.
Like the journalist who actually saw the sea serpent, I
realized that dredging the dictionary for adjectives
would only make this tale of a Repertory success less
credible; simple words were the best. Still, that I
might not seem to lag behind my colleagues in enthusiasm, I had sent for all the morning papers to know the
utmost of their caracoling, only to find that, at its highest, Miss Thorndike's press was sober-gaited. Gloomy—
sordid—sombre—depressing—a bet to make us miserable: the procession was uniformly grey. Only Mr.
Baughan, whose sword-hand I grasp, pronounced *Jane
Clegg* a happy choice.

I would ask those gentlemen who were rendered
gloomy and depressed, whether for a bet or otherwise,
what actually they demand. They have rid Miss Thorndike of the strangulations of Grand Guignol. For whole
seasons together they have deplored, with reason, the
insincerity of the " commercial " play, and, with eyes
raised to Heaven, have demanded, " How long, O Lord,
how long? " And now that the good thing has
descended they are dissatisfied. Stoutly, and with the
knowledge that one faithful spirit is with me, I maintain
that the production of this play at the New Theatre is
the best thing that has befallen the English stage for a
very long time. Oh, you public, who flock to monstrous
ineptitudes in the face of your best-revered critics, flout
them once again! I have torn up my beautiful article

56

A Lance for Jane

for you; not for me, but for your own sakes, go to see this play! "Is it a fine work?" used to be the foyer's question. "Is it a winner?" is the query of our more vulgar age. Admitted that not even a critic likes to back consistent losers, the point is that, in this case, my favourite is a real good horse. Miss Thorndike has apparently come tandem-wise to town, that steady goer "Repertory" in the wheel, light-hearted "Grand Guignol" frisking in the lead. But there is nothing of the patient, weary mare about *Jane Clegg*. In horse parlance she does more than plod; she trots on. In a way I understand the dubiety of the critics with regard to work ostentatiously labelled "repertory." They have not forgotten the recent pronouncement of the melancholy gentleman in direful Carey Street. "This venture," said the official receiver, with reference to the affairs of the precedent Everyman Theatre, Limited, "was foredoomed to failure, owing to the public taking no interest in it." A saying hard as that of the apologist who sought to defend a peculiarly exorbitant massacre on the ground that if a race will hold an unpopular faith it should know what to expect. In other words, "I'll larn thee to be a toad!"

Well, the critics ought not to want to "larn" Miss Thorndike to be an intellectual actress. It is now sixteen or seventeen years since I saw this queen of repertory at Miss Horniman's theatre in Manchester; and surely there never lighted on that stage, which none but the earnest might tread, a more fervent vision. I saw her just above the horizon, decorating and cheering. . . . Here my little *pastiche* comes to a conscientious stop. Not even Burke himself could pretend that

A Lance for Jane

the Jane Cleggs, the Barthwicks, and other *dejeÉta membra* of the Manchester Gaiety's dispiriting sister-hood were decorative or cheerful. Not from the faint nebula of repertory did ever great aÉtor spring, " glitter-ing like the morning star, full of life, and splendour, and joy." In the conStellations of pure fuStian has he always shone. But is it not possible that we are about to change all that ? The performance at the New Theatre inclines me to think so.

The essence of modern play-writing is truth to life, of modern aÉting that it shall refuse to portray human beings as satellites revolving round some monStrous-seeming sun. Our fathers, seeking not truth but fire-works, looked to behold in their chief aÉtor an orb so dazzling that when, for the nonce, he disappeared behind clouds obsequiously gathering againSt his next glorious dispersal, his attendant fellows were veiled in a green diStress. We encourage this old failing when we insiSt that the public cannot be intereSted in good plays, desiring only to see good aÉtors. That never the twain shall meet is untrue; they meet in this play. That *Jane Clegg* is a title of discouragement I will not deny. Melancholy dissyllable of sound, unison to Poor Jo and every eleemosynary appellation under Heaven! At its tolling the critics betake themselves to wondering what profane enchantment the layman, lacking the artiSt's delight in craftsmanship, will find in this drama of ways and means. Poverty is notoriously hateful and degrad-ing, the root of all evil. The poor man, say the critics, has the subjeÉt by heart, and finds no delight in its aeSthetic treatment. He is, in point of faÉt, not inter-eSted in the playwright's guesses. He knows! Did not

A Lance for Jane

Sir Arthur Pinero realize this when he declared drama to be impossible in establishments of less than two thousand a year ? A beggarly seven hundred pounds is all the capital of the Cleggs, and that the property of Jane. What possibility of drama here ?

Now let me ask these depressed and critical gentlemen what they would have said of a presentation by Sir Arthur of Mr. St. John Ervine's theme. Let them first consider how he would have turned it.

Jane, Duchess of Cleggshire, refuses her millions, not to her dishonest clerk of a husband, but to a ducal director conniving at the rascalities of his board. His Grace's blackmailer is no pettifogging bookmaker's tout, but an owner of racehorses; his fancy woman no drab, but a *diva* of Continental misrepute. The third act is gracefully disposed about the shores of Como; talk there is of *loggias* and *piazzas*, with cognizant domestics bandying such significances as *Che farò?* and *Una furtiva lagrima*, in preparation for the great scene in which, to get her man back, the Duchess shall presently pipe her eye. (I cannot decide, off-hand, whether Sir Arthur's Duchess would have wept her Duke over, or taken a header from the balcony; the particular upshot is no matter.)

Doubtless the dramatist would have fulfilled one important function of the theatre, which is to hold the mirror up to an expensive side of life which nine-tenths of the audience can never know. But let me ask the critics whether, after paying tribute to Sir Arthur's technique, they would not have deplored his " insincerity." Would they not have expressed themselves as *depressed* by these costly villegiatourists ? Why not

59

A Lance for Jane

Hammersmith? they would have sighed. Well, here *is* Hammersmith!

Here, too, is truth. I know nothing more absolutely true than Henry Clegg's final apology. In it this shiftless, insubstantial fellow—a masterpiece of acting by Mr. Leslie Faber, perfect in insight and technique from the cunning, shallow mentality to the greasy locks curling over the low forehead—poured out the bottom of his greasy, furtive soul. " I'm not a bad chap, really. I'm just weak. I'd be all right if I had a lot of money and a wife that wasn't better than I am. . . . Oh, I know, Jane! You *are* better than I am. Any fool can see that! It doesn't do a chap much good to be living with a woman who's his superior, at least, not the sort of chap I am. I ought to have married a woman like myself, or a bit worse. That's what Kitty is. She's worse than I am, and that sort of makes me love her. It's different with you. I always feel mean here. Yes, I am mean. I know that; but it makes me meaner than I really am to be living with you."

Such a coda does not depress me; nor yet does the play which it recapitulates. Rather does it bring about in me a solemn exultation. I should have thought ten thousand critical swords must have leapt from their scabbards at the suggestion that *Jane Clegg* is a dull play. Alas that the swords had no choice. Their wearers glued their hands to the pommel and swore the thing was dull. Let me make this concession that those who look to the drama for after-dinner entertainment will not find here that which they seek. To any plea that such a play searches, sears, and scarifies the Henry Cleggs sitting in the audience they reply, with some justice, that

A Lance for Jane

the theatre is not meant for a house of correction; that, forewarned, these frail vessels had betaken themselves to a place of lesser shock. In plain blunt English, no Henry Clegg of the upper classes willingly puts down twelve shillings and sixpence to have his soul dragged from him and publicly carpet-beaten. There is a good deal in this. The age of hair-shirts is gone, and it is doubtful if they were ever fashionable for exterior wear. That of "sophisters, œconomists, and calculators" has succeeded. Let her who is already a great actress be wise in her time and generation. Let her look not upon masterpieces only. Let her know that there be those among her admirers who are not content to watch her sitting at a table darning socks for three mortal hours on end. The turn of her head on the word "Judas!" is, to me, worth a wilderness of Toscas. Yet to many it is not worth so much as a single shudder of that distraught lady. In the theatre, be it remembered, paste is more effective than diamonds. Sybil—the fine flowers of the stage should be unipetalous—will do well from time to time to flaunt her Toscas, Fédoras, Adriennes. Let her not care that this sort of thing does not find her at her best. It would not be fair that intellectual actresses, deprived of the opportunity of being intellectual, should vie with their nonsensical sisters. I once saw Eleonora Duse in *Adrienne Lecouvreur*, and it seemed to me that, in a single evening, Sarah had paid off all outstanding intellectual scores. Let not Sybil disdain to plunge her august nose into that old-fashioned bouquet. I who, when she essays these high priestesses of Bamboozledom, am not illuded, promise to shut my eyes. And, closing them, I will indulge in other dreams, perchance of that first act of

61

A Lance for Jane

The Maid's Tragedy, in which she poured forth enough bitter satirical largesse to defray the comic expenditure of half the fashionable actresses in London throughout an entire year. I will blind me to her occasional rubbish against the day when she shall blaze forth in what succession of masterpieces she will. And thou— forgive, sweet poet—and thou, beautiful goddess, in that far time, when in thy triumph sweet thou gazest down, wilt thou remember that once I fought for thee, breaking a lance for Jane?

Art and the Screen

ET ME CONFESS THAT I CANNOT make up my mind about the film called *Way Down East*. The theatre proper seldom finds me in any quandary, alas! beyond that imposed in the choice between nonsense and rubbish; the difficulty about this production of D. W. Griffiths is that I know what I think about it absolutely, but not relatively. Absolutely it is, with one exception, the best " picture " I have seen; how high we should place the best achievement of the screen is another matter. The need for circumspection was borne in upon me by the answers of three of my friends whom I invited to assist my judgment. The first desired that evening to finish a book by Marcel Proust; the second was engaged to hear a Brahms Symphony; the third telegraphed curtly, " Never go to films."

The implication that the film cannot be considered a form of art is, I am sure, utterly wrong. Art is not an immutable thing, rigidly contained within fixed laws. The principle of beauty may be unalterable; its expression must keep pace with mechanical invention. Those who wilfully deny the aesthetic possibilities of the film seem to me to belong to the slightly demented order of beings who would go back to printing in black letter, hand-loom weaving, the viol da gamba, and the toga. Art stopped short neither with the Empress Josephine nor with Mr. Edison. What a mess of it

Art and the Screen

serious composers would have made if they had stopped resolutely at the harpsichord and ignored the piano! The piano was bound to come, and the artist could best defend it from the vulgar by using it himself. So, too, the cinema had to come, and our dramatists can best preserve this new medium of drama from the clowns by utilizing it themselves. Synchronization is in the air, and I am persuaded that the operatic composer will do well to consider the screen-scenario as the peg upon which he must, sooner or later, hang his score. The authors of drama and of music-drama may as well compose themselves to the situation first as last, since, like Mrs. Bardell, to this situation they must come. It is inevitable. It is inevitable because the screen is a medium which the clowns, so far from exhausting, cannot even adequately fill. All art is the depicting of emotion; the art of the theatre should be obedience in one form or another to the primal behest, " Tell me, or show me, or make me hear a story." The story may be of shipwreck on some desert isle, or of bournes faintly discoverable to the spirit, but it remains essentially a story. Art, we may safely say, can never be divorced from some form of remembered experience. The screen presents that experience, or story, more directly, more nakedly, than any other medium. All other forms of art proceed by means of clothing; so that you behold not the facts but tailoring. But there are many simple folk who can read life and not books, who can put two and two together so long as they are allowed to do it for themselves. They resent the artist, who for them gets in the way. A girl lost in a snowstorm and her lover in search of her need no comment. They make up a

Art and the Screen

page in a book which anybody may read without the trouble of learning to spell. Now if the screen delighted none but the illiterate we could afford to leave it to the buffoons. Since, however, my own emotion tells me that in proper hands it is capable of affording intense aesthetic delight, we cannot so abandon it.

The cinema is undoubtedly the biggest educational event since the invention of printing. Its appeal is wider than that even of music; Eskimo and Hottentot may not hear artificial sound-patterns with our ears, but at least they must see actual happenings with our eyes. Millions, were they suddenly deprived of the cinema, would feel its loss more than that of the printing-press. (Symbols could always be arranged to show the winner of the two-thirty.) Millions have been captured by the cinema in ten years, whose imagination has been untouched by five hundred years of the written word and three thousand of the spoken. If the cinema were fitted for none but boors, the question of its use might well remain an economic one. I would maintain that we can no more proclaim its ultimate accomplishment than the man who first accidentally banged his fist against a stretched goat-skin could foretell his. Be it remembered, too, that unlike all the other arts the cinema has not had the advantage of slow growth. It was a pure mechanical invention, sprung suddenly upon the type of mind most antithetical to that of the artist, one which had the additional disability of being American. " I think," said Hogarth to Horace Walpole, " it is owing to the good sense of the English that they have not painted better." I think it is owing to the vulgarity of Americans that they have filmed so sentimentally.

Art and the Screen

The English painter tried to turn sterling sense into poetry, the American producer knew that he could in no way transfigure the search for the almighty dollar. And so launched upon the sentimentality which nauseates. *Way Down East* does not contain one ounce of sentimentality; it is, however, full of sentiment. Mr. D. W. Griffiths in this film has realized many things. He has realized that an art, of which the essence is the non-interference of the artist, will tell the simple stories best. His theme of seduction is as simply treated as in "Adam Bede," though I would not have you infer that Mr. William Brady, the original author, has a mind as big as George Eliot's. In Hetty's case, you remember, there was not the concession of the mock marriage. Mr. Griffiths has realized that tawdriness comes with trivial ornament. In allowing his story to tell itself, he has shown himself a master of avoidances.

But this producer has virtues more positive. He has that which allows you to dwell upon things intrinsically beautiful, so that the mind has time to impregnate itself with beauty and attain to that disposition in which cold, substantial facts begin to glow with warm, insubstantial meaning. The artist, one may think, is no more than a preparer of the mind, one in whose presence you wring from facts not their significance, not even his interpretation, but your own very special sense of their meaning and beauty. So in this simple instance of art by photography the mind is allowed to make what it will of a bunch of lilac, a bird pecking a girl's cheek, a jollification in a country inn. It is possible that the sophisticated have thought their fill of these simple things, that they are more dependent than the unlettered upon the interpretations of others. If this be so, I see nothing in the love-making by the river to prevent me from harking back to that passage which begins, " Pipe, happy sheep-boy, love! " There is no reason, except that her " trouble " is over instead of being to come, why I should not re-create in that little figure trudging the unending road that poor wretch who, in one of Hardy's novels, drags herself from mile-post to mile-post. Nor yet why the festivities at the farm should not remind me of Mr. Wardle's. I do not say that these borrowings are necessary; I do say that some transmutation of these simple things is possible, in one's own mind if it comes to the pinch. The fineness of the ultimate gold depends upon the fineness of the mind which does the transmuting. The sea-change into coral and pearl depends from the magic of the sea.

There is, in this film, that keen differentiation of character, whereby each figure stands out so that you can raise it, in the general process of metamorphosis, to an abstract quality. Thus the Squire becomes Intolerance and the gossip Tittle-Tattle. There is the musical illustration, a " Sinfonia Domestica " of remembered ballads, of themes which would bespeak jollity if carved on a frieze, of appropriate silences. There is the great thrill of the ice-floe. These, singly, are admirable. They could have been put together so that their sum had been without meaning. The picture as I saw it—twice on successive days—moves me strangely; pro-portion and rhythm, which together are the foundation of all art, must have gone to the making of this film as surely as to that volume of Proust which my friend desired to finish. The crux of the matter is not to what

Art and the Screen

extent a particular film is pathetic or amusing, but to decide whether we may include even the best film within the scope and category of art. I think, definitely, that in this case we may, and that in the case of such a picture as *Broken Blossoms* we must. *Way Down East* seems to me to be a less good film than *Broken Blossoms*, because it lacks that strangeness of beauty which Pater marked off from order in beauty. Yet it has the compensations of order, its characters being among those " who soon as we are born, are straight our friends." It is less good because it lacks the Whistlerian fogs and shadows of that setting, and that dock in Limehouse ever recurring like some pedal point. I once read an Eastern poem of but a single line

" Oh, these wistaria flowers! "

some of the ache and beauty of which Richard Bartelmess got into his performance of the Chinese boy. His part in *Way Down East* hardly admits of distinction. Here, too, Lilian Gish cannot be more than fragrant in gentleness and woe, though her scene with the dead child is most moving. Whereas that other picture shows that she possesses the power without which we must not use the word " genius." And use it of this actress I do, deliberately. How like Sarah she can look! It is curious that, when she lets her hair fall down the sides of her pinched, woe-begone face, with all the expressiveness of that wistful countenance drawn from the eyes down the long suspense of the nose, to come to final meaning in the trembling mouth—it is curious that this plain little American child should give the world an exact image of the great actress in her far-off youth.

Dear Barrie

Dear Brutus, by J. M. Barrie. Wyndham's Theatre.

ONCE THERE WAS A MOTHER STAR gathered little baby stars round her knee to tell them a fairy-story, and during the telling the genius of Barrie was born. For genius it is, despite a passion for literary baby-ribbons only too easily parodied. You could never mistake *Dear Brutus*, recently revived at Wyndham's Theatre, for the accretion of a talent, however industrious. The rarer attribute is written all over it, not very large perhaps, but in the authentic handwriting. The essence of genius is its power to achieve without pains. That *tour de force* of Jupiter's, the birth of Minerva, was the trick, unrehearsed and inimitable. None but the old gentleman would have thought of it. It is surely the hall-mark of genius that its fruits, but for their creator, had never been thought of. Talent plods, and its outcome will be stumbled upon sooner or later, if not by the first explorer then by another. A later than Newton would have questioned the falling apple, a second Stephenson drawn deductions from his kettle. Einstein merely anticipated by a week or a century the inevitable discovery that nothing's white or black but relativity makes it so. Something of the sort had just occurred to me. In the world of talent it is " dogged as does it." In the world of genius it is dogged as doesn't.

Dear Barrie

To come to our little organism called the theatre. Can it be doubted that if Sir Arthur Pinero or Mr. John Drinkwater had turned their great talents away from the stage, we should still have had *The Second Mrs. Tanqueray* or *Abraham Lincoln*? Their epochs reeked with these plays. Non-existent, their temper was in the air. If St. Paul had lived in the 'nineties he would have pursued the lady with whips, scorpions, and perhaps an even fuller understanding; regenerate, he would have mouthed those melancholy confidences, enlivening them, it may be, with a dash of the original Saul. But he would never, we must think, have hit upon Peter Pan, or the boy who "bit his warts and politely swallowed the blood." Not even a greater genius can recapture the lost spirit of a lesser. Hartmann defines this quality as "the spontaneous manifestation of the untrammelled soul," but then he was a German. To the non-Teutonic mind it is obvious that genius must take some pains; it were inspired lunacy else. So Beethoven tinkers incessantly at his themes, with the result that after twenty years he has whittled his chromatic glory down to the diatonic monotony apt for the plastering of Schiller's "Ode to Joy." Contrariwise we find Dickens hammering a grotesque name on the anvil till he has forged the apparently inspired "Chuzzlewit." Like these, Barrie is no wander-wit, but a master-contriver. His soul, as Herbert says, may be divinely loose about him, but he makes fast with the shrewdest nails such bits of it as he uses. Yet it is only the form of the conceit which he fashions into shape; the raw material of felicity springs from his brain flushed with ultimate delight.

A reviewer of the early *Little Minister* wrote, " The

Dear Barrie

reader is held spell-bound, not by any cunningly devised artifices, but by the sympathy which is evoked in his breaſt." That which held the reviewer spell-bound was, of course, the sympathy overflowing in the writer's breaſt. Sir James himself has said a good deal on this matter of sympathy. The Dominie asks Sentimental Tommy how he managed to write the passage about the willow hanging over the grave. " I thought I was Betsy at the time," answered Tommy. " She told me nothing about the willow," countered Mr. Cathro. " You hadna speired if there was one," the boy retorted. There you have both the natural gift, and the painſtaker's looking before and after. " Oh, you jewel! " cried Mr. Ogilvy, when Tommy lost the essay prize through excessive deliberation over the juſt word. " He *had* to think of it till he got it. The laddie is a genius! " Which looks as though Sir James held, as they say, with Ecclefechan. The word was at the back of Tommy's mind all the time; the infinity of pains was used to bring it to the surface. The peculiar genius of Barrie, as playwright, consiſts in his knack of bringing from the back of his mind the simple things which lie behind the mind of the speƈtator. They are the things which, but for the twiſt of kindly laughter, would be unbearable. For the same reason Barrie prefers sentimentality to sentiment, because it hurts less. Fortitude, irony even, are plants too prickly for his tender world. To keep young is the great adventure; old age and death are but dream-disaſters. " To be very gay is so near to being very sad," is as near to aƈtuality as Sir James will venture. I know of no other writer who has burked life so exquisitely.

Dear Barrie

It is a mistake to regard genius as entirely magnoperative. It has its small change. *Dear Brutus* resembles nothing so much as a miser's hoard of newly-minted threepenny-bits. Or say that it is a collection of entire and perfect sugar-plums. Success has over-sweetened this writer, sicklied his philosophy with the pink cast of sugar-icing, choked up his manliness with the clotted cream of nursery kindness. What would we not give for a compunctious visiting of reality, a kindly touch of gall ? Yet this is an age of ugliness and we may suppose the pretty-pretty, when the heart's sound, to serve a useful purpose. I had never seen this play, and expected, from remembered accounts of it, to be as intolerably moved as I was by *Mary Rose*. To be quite honest, I did not find my sensibility greatly touched. This failure was no fault of the playing, which could not have been better. Miss Faith Celli, who had a hundred opportunities to be irritating or purposefully charming, which is the same thing, avoided them all. She managed that very delicate business of wistfulness admirably, and at the same time made you feel that she was capable of playing a useful game of hockey for her school. She was brilliantly helped by Sir Gerald du Maurier, who played the sentimental father with extraordinary tact. Let those who say this delicate player does not act, note how nice is the quantity of emotion conveyed when the father wakes to the loss of his dream-child. Note, too, the subtlety of his earlier degradation, and the moral well-being of the painter in the wood. You would swear the good fellow subscribes to " Punch," and that the picture on the easel is not altogether bad. Throughout the long duet father and daughter maintained the atmosphere of a dream. Unreality floated about them like wisps of summer cloud. And yet . . . and yet I was not fully absorbed. The material was juſt not good enough. Visions of a Mr. Tucker who, on the music-halls, sings to the accompaniment of a fiddle played by himself a song entitled, " The Land of Beginning Again," would come between me and the players. I remembered that the momentum achieved by Mr. Tucker was just as great as theirs. Again, when the little lady crucified herself againſt the tree, I could not help murmuring, " Look on my face; my name is Might-have-been," and wondering where the line comes from. And who was it, in " Alice," who fell into the treacle-well ? Whereas, at *Mary Rose* the emotional tension precluded irrelevant preoccupation. In that play Sir James wore his heart juſt as patently, but it seemed more effeɕtively; and the critical daws averted their eyes. The other night I found the daw which is in all of us the leaſt bit inclined to be peckish. Again it cannot have been the fault of the aɕtors. Mr. Norman Forbes who, " when suited," as they say in regiſtry offices, so handsomely repays his author, was at his very beſt, whilſt Mr. Alfred Drayton's Matey was both maſterful and maſterly. I think it is Trollope who apologizes for laying the scene of a novel in Ireland. Sir James and Mr. Ronald Squire made sure between them that there should be nothing Scotch about *Dear Brutus*. The aɕtor's Mr. Purdie was labelled " England 1912 or thereabouts," as legibly as though it had been emblazoned on his shirt-front. Here again was a charaɕter with limitless potentialities of annoyance. Mr. Squire overcame them all and abounded in the airs of the well-bred scapegrace. The beauty of Miss Madeleine Seymour had the effect of a great splash of colour, and the tenderness of Miss Mabel Terry Lewis gathered about her scenes like some veil of exquisite *vieux rose*.

Two Ways of Being Earnest

Justice, by John Galsworthy. Everyman Theatre.
Fanny's First Play, by Bernard Shaw. Court Theatre.

AN EVENING PAPER BEARING THE date of the revival of *Justice* at the Everyman Theatre, or of *Fanny's First Play*, at the Court —it is unimportant which—contained an article dealing with a murder trial of some years ago. One sentence bore upon a subject which was not for that jury. " The action in this case unrolls itself in a milieu, which not only suggests the theatre, but seems hardly conceivable as existing in modern London."

Now " milieu," boiled down, means people. One wondered whether the writer, who declared himself a barrister and a Bachelor of Arts, and appeared possessed of the lawyer's sense of logic, recognized the full impli- cation of that " not only." Must the theatre concern itself only with people who don't exist ? Not Jeremy Collier, in his " Short View " of what the English stage was up to in his time, not Mr. Shaw in his lengthiest disquisition as to what it might and should be up to in ours, has hit off prevailing conditions with a nicer contempt. That our West End playwrights care nothing for real people is true; that Mr. Shaw and Mr. Galsworthy care enormously is equally true. But with this remarkable difference, that whereas the Gals- worthian butcher, baker, candlestick-maker retains his own mentality, the Shavian linen-draper wears the same cast of mind as his author's. It is the social accident which puts the clerk in the dock instead of his employer; it is Mr. Shaw's whim that Fanny writes the play instead of her father's footman. Mr. Galsworthy's people "keep their place"; Mr. Shaw's know only his. The creatures of both are tremendously alive in the sense that to their creators they are at once real and, in the proper sense, tremendous. One dramatist is fearful of external buffetings, or man's inhumanity to man; the other fears only man's inhumanity to himself. To the sentimental Englishman proneness to self-deception is both natural and human; to the logical Irishman it is unnatural and inhuman. Mr. Galsworthy has no spark of humour; Mr. Shaw jokes because he is so tremendously and fearfully in earnest.

It has not, I think, been claimed for this philosopher-wit that he has exposed his own theory of Relativity. Relativity is no bogey. In the natural world it means no more than that it is the event which is the truth, and that matter, space, and time are the language in which we express that event. But so long ago as 1911 Mr. Shaw was writing: "Mere morality, or the substitution of custom for conscience, was once accounted a shameful and cynical thing: people talked of right and wrong, of honour and dishonour, of sin and grace, of salvation and damnation, not of morality and immorality." It is the event, you see, which exists, whilst morality is the language in which we discuss it. The author talks in his preface about making his young people shed their respectability and put on self-respect. What he does in *Fanny's First Play* is to put them into the police-court.

Two Ways of Being Earnest

Once more Mr. Shaw sets the straightforward, simple-minded evil-doer above the righteous fellow who will not be honest in his chatter. It is impossible for a play with such a theme to grow old. That which was at any time fresh in it must remain fresh. It dates only in inessentials, though these may vary in significance. Young womanhood has made enormous strides in experience during the last ten years. Women who have won through to the suffrage and careered honourably and steadfastly over a Europe at war, are not likely to be staggered by Margaret Knox's exploit on Boat Race night. Frequenters of the cheaper music-halls no longer drink champagne. Mrs. Gilbey to-day pays more for her lace. These things do not matter. What does, and must always matter, is Margaret's defiant: " I didn't do it for a lark, I did it out of the very depths of my nature. I did it because I'm that sort of person. I did it in one of my religious fits."

This fine declaration, couched in terms of laughter, not because of some kink of perversity, but because Englishmen will not allow the theatre to talk morality except in the form of a joke, could have been written by Shaw only, and by no one else. It is incredible that when the play was produced anonymously, this apparently flippant, yet wholly serious, confession unto salvation did not instantly give away the author. Shaw is manifest not only here, but in every line—in the ecstasy of redemption none the less fervent because the redeeming is to be of this world, in the surge of common sense, in the mischievous juxtaposition of the salvationist and the baggage, in the poverty of incident and prolixity of mere talk, even in the queer megalomania of it all. Never

77

Two Ways of Being Earnest

very good jokes, the induction and epilogue are to-day quite exquisitely boring. Mr. Shaw entertains us less when he is guying Mr. Trotter, the Cambridge Fabian Society, or himself, than when he is in deadly earnest about life. It is his quality of seriousness which matters, and if, in this pleasant farce, you fail to catch the spirit of old Bunyan blowing through the Shavian trumpet, you are in for a dull time. The play would not be worth reviving if it were not for Margaret's declaration and the hint that the feather-brained little trull, Dora, is as good a mate as another for that normal, likeable little cad, Bobby. But that the play has its unamusing reaches and backwaters, those who know their Shaw best will best know. When, in the third act, the quartet got its argumentative knees under the mahogany I wanted to run away. My newspaper contained, in addition to the murder case, an account of a young man who had been tried for the rare crime of breaking out of church. Long before the quartet, with the help of the Frenchman, had settled its differences, I wanted to break out of the Everyman Theatre. Would it never end ? Only, I reflected, at this playhouse they lock the doors.

Where Mr. Shaw would give you something to break your mind upon, Mr. Galsworthy invites you to break your heart. Perhaps we may admit that *Justice* is not a fine play because it brought about a measure of prison reform. To teach the justiciary his business is not the concern of the artist. The play contains less of pure thought and more of pure emotion than any other of these sterling melodramas. A pure thinker would not, one imagines, have based a general plea upon so indi-

78

vidual and sympathetic a case as Falder. How would
our other playwright have revelled, not in this weakling,
but in a criminal possessing the courage of his crime!
Can we not imagine Fanny's double-barrelled defence—
first that her criminal was not a criminal at all and, in the
alternative, that vindictive punishment is wrong, even in
the case of the most hardened scoundrels? Fanny
would have begun this second play where she began
her first, at the point where the gaoler lets go. All that
precedes is deeply moving and " makes a good play,"
but it is not to any particular philosophic point. But if
the " sense of the theatre " is what is wanted, then this is
fine drama. We could do with another three hours of it.
We want to explore farther into the relations of Falder
and Ruth, with all that has gone before laid bare, to hear
what that dull fellow, the employer, thinks of the consequences of prosecution, to learn what case society may
make for its protection. There must be a better one
than Mr. Galsworthy puts up. In this play he is a
cozening figure of Justice, with eyes unbandaged, scales
liberally weighted with compassion, the sword-edge
turned towards the rich. The two revivals show these
writers in admirable contrast, Shaw the intellectual
pioneer navvying speculation with pick and shovel,
Galsworthy the orderer of such thought as we already
possess. The one is all " flash and outbreak of a fiery
mind," the other a lamp of pity. But there is a sense in
which neither can hold a candle to the other.

Another Essay on the Comic Spirit

"A DIRTY MIND," DECLARED THE Dook Snook in "Ally Sloper's Half-Holiday," "is a perpetual feaſt." This is a motto which, had I my way, would be emblazoned over the portals of every music-hall in the kingdom. Only I should probably inscribe the word "healthy," and rely upon your Pantagrueliſt, who alone should be free of these temples, to catch at the Rabelaisian sense. The music-hall is emphatically no place for the nice-minded, the makers of finical diſtinctions. It is essentially a place for the catholic. The great virtue of Rabelais is that he writes openly of those things which are commonly relegated to the privies of the mind. The great virtue of the music-hall is that it jokes openly of those things which are commonly discussed in bar-parlours. Whenever this openness is in any degree veiled, we descend at once to that "durtie hypocrisie," which is the supreme offence.

These very obvious reflections are suggeſted by recent performances, at the Holborn Empire, of a music-hall artiſt to whom I am devoted, Miss May Henderson, and, at the Victoria Palace, of another artiſt to whom I am not devoted at all. Miss Henderson, the "Dusky Comedy Queen," makes no appeal to the dissembling mind. She provokes no furtive snigger. Her wit is not "near the knuckle"; it is the knuckle itself.

80

Another Essay on the Comic Spirit

The only possible excuse for her rib-ticklers is their outspokenness. Like Rabelais, her joking may be occasionally concerned with foul things, but it is never indecent. She " drags away the veil with a strong hand, does not leave impropriety half-covered and so prompt the reader (spectator) to a filthy curiosity." In addition to its humour, the performance of this artist is of the highest technical excellence. Her songs go with the rattle of machine-guns. There was one ecstatic moment when every person in the theatre proclaimed himself, with a huge shout, to be of the untrammelled company of Pantagruel. The only exceptions were those whose youth, as Stevenson quaintly says, had been depressed by exceptional aesthetic surroundings. Of such I glimpsed but two.

The quality of that other performance, at the Victoria Palace, was quite different. Superficially of a higher order of " gentility," it offended against Pantagruelism in that it provoked the imagination without intent to satisfy. The artist, who was enormously stout, made exhibition of a great deal of bare flesh. As a minor compensation she had the wit to provoke you to think she would not have resented comparison with Beardsley's drawing of the women in " The Wagnerites." Now there is no harm in bare flesh, but there is harm in jokes about nakedness—the harm of commonness. In its essence this was a performance for kitchen-maids. One does not resent kitchen maids; they are useful people, and are entitled to entertainment. What one did resent was the *décor*, the expensiveness of such clothes as there were, the grand piano, the " drawing-room atmosphere." *Facetiae* fittingly babbled over a slop-stone, or

Another Essay on the Comic Spirit

among bellying clothes-lines, were out of place here. At the Holborn Empire I had been less displeased by a child of, apparently, some seven summers, in baby-bonnet and baby-socks, delivering herself of such sophistications as

> " There's a tavern in the town, in the town,
>   And it's my town,
>   It's not a dry town;
> I shall take my pals and my pa and ma
> To have a drop of whiskey in the old back bar,
> When I get back to my town, to my town."

This was nauseating, but at least the mind was untouched. Whereas what one felt about the grown-up performance was that it directly encouraged the grocer's assistant and the butcher's boy, if not to a more vicious way of living, at least to a commoner way of thinking.

In justice to the young gentleman in dress clothes who had helped to crack the jokes about nudity, let me record that when he was left to his own devices he sang, and sang very well, the good ballad, " Johnny Ludlow," and that the resultant applause was ten times greater than that evoked by his quips to lechery. The programme included Mr. G. S. Melvin, " The Versatile Comedian." Mr. Melvin did not strike me as being a comedian at all, but rather as an actor of exceedingly clever invention. It is no small feat to impersonate a figure of Bakst, a ship's stoker, and a bluestocking at a University Extension lecture, all to the life and within half an hour. The bluestocking was really a man attired for bathing, and stucco'd, as to the legs, like some prehistoric monster of Mr. E. T. Reed, but there was on his startled countenance the ingratiating expression of the earnest female peering through pince-nez at improving truth. The stoker was remarkably true to life. Mr. Melvin is almost as graceful a dancer as Eugene Stratton, and it is a pity that he winds up some admirable acting with a poverty-stricken, sentimental song. There were also Mr. Fred Karno's comedians in *Mumming Birds*, at once a burlesque and the very stuff of the music-hall. One of the comic gentlemen gave an " impression " of Sir Frank Benson as Mark Antony. " Sir Frank " forgot his words and substituted, not some happy froth blown Shakespeareanly about the surface of this actor's temperament, but a line from a well-known chorus of Miss Florrie Ford.

Mr. Ainley's appearance at The Palladium in a dramatic sketch entitled *Talma* drew from one critic the majestic aspiration that this fine actor might woo this audience from its admiration of tumblers and comedians. This attitude seems to me entirely mistaken. To laugh at the humour of the red nose is proper to the after-dinner man. Tumblers, with their swift wheeling and diving, take even the replete mind with beauty. Or, if you insist that your pleasure shall be ratiocinatory, those practical philosophers, the Pasquali Brothers, will set you reflecting that, as between equilibrists, Newton and not another holds the gravitational field. The Pasqualis achieved exactly that which they proposed. They did not leave you to think, as Talma and his interlocutors did, how much better it would have been if you could have heard what they said. Their performance was not lumbering like the prose of Mr.

Another Essay on the Comic Spirit

Henry Hertz, nor wavering like his playlet's sentiment, nor short of the mark like Talma's acting with nobody to play up to, nor wide of it like the magnoperations of this tragic fish out of water. Mr. Ainley's Talma is a good imitative shot at the grand tradition. But when I am in a music-hall I resent the usurpation, by an actor howsoever great, of space which were more appropriately filled by Mr. Harry Weldon. Homer never wrote fasting, and Cato never wrote till after he had drunk, says Rabelais. Neither, I am sure, would have visited the Palladium until he had both eaten and drunk. Whereas I would take my stand, fasting, in a queue a mile long before any proper theatre which should announce:

Shakespeare's Tragedy
of
KING RICHARD III
Richard, Duke of Gloucester . . . Mr. Ainley.

See to it, Hal. My king! My Jove! I speak to thee, my heart! So do I interpret the applause of the Palladium audience. They appreciated Mr. Ainley's quality, though they had difficulty in deciding what, exactly, it was concerned with; they apprehended that here was the stamp of great acting, but hoped the actor would not unduly delay the funny fellows. Mr. Ainley's interposition among clowns was as disturbing to that audience as, doubtless to the reader, the intrusion of hunch-back'd Gloucester in an essay which began with Ally Sloper. I can only plead that the readjustment here necessitated is not more violent than that which I had to perform, unaided, after the death-throes of Talma.

Another Essay on the Comic Spirit

I have never seen anything quite so realistic as *The Rest Cure*, a playlet at the Holborn Empire. In five minutes I knew that here was a masterpiece. A sick man in pyjamas, carrying his boots and balancing a silk hat on the top of a red and touzled wig, suggests the comic as Mr. Karno's comedians understand it. And, indeed, the invalid's antics are of that order. But they are built up on ideas, wee intellectual mice running about the foot of a mountain of grosser folly. There is the nurse who never comes into the room without insisting upon making up the bed. There is the solicitous friend whose newspaper opens at the story " Sad Death in a Nursing Home. Damp Sheets the Cause." We know, in dreams of farce wilder than the stage may give, that mourner who, taking the sleeper for dead, cannot decide how to dispose his flowers to advantage about the body, and that undertaker's man who, having taken his melancholy measure, finds his tape to be *wider* than the door. That these things should be so little funny on paper is good evidence of their theatrical effectiveness when you couple them with the fact that they sent the house into delirium. Each of the actors possessed an enormous sense of character. They were not just buffoons, but *buffo* incarnations of the sinister. In their funereal garb they stood out like puppets in a marionette show; and their actions took on all the super-consequence of puppets. Or you could liken them to those unfortunate attorneys, singing-masters, pantaloons who, in Rossinian opera, are eternally fated to be thrust out of doors. There was thoughtful laughter here as well as pictorial burlesque. " Where did those flowers come from ? " asked the aggrieved patient. "A bookmaker brought them!" replied the man of shrouds, preoccupied with his tape and that all too narrow door.

When I arrived at the Princes Theatre it was to find the house in delighted uproar over a comedy of manners performed by the Brothers Griffiths, than whom Mr. Shaw declared the late James Welch could never be funnier. It was a question of a sleight-of-hand performance to which the more robust of the brothers, in the genteel get-up of a theatrical manager, was making conscientious objection. Perched upon that round, bullet-like head, and significant of " the front of the house " was the authentic topper, a shade too small. But only a shade. The discrepancy, less than that connoted by caricaturists of Mr. Churchill and Mr. George, was, indeed, of an extraordinary *vraisemblance.* The cylinder posed as coping-stone of the man of small successes, of one who has a snug sum put by. *Finis coronat opus.* The tile crowned a life-work. Yet was all not well. The least spark of argumentative heat, and the hat would take a tilt over the nose to the extinction of rebuke. A gesture imperfectly restrained, and it would slither rearwards to discover a witless cranium. This dressy fellow and enforced equilibrist must walk delicately, with haviour protestant yet static. Now adjustment is slight, now it gives place to magnoperative retrieval. Reiterant, the disputant picks up the thread of his discourse. He gets a sentence well under weigh and his countenance relaxes into security. He rounds his period and starts with confidence on the next. But his certainty is ill-founded; he had done better to heed the famous advice of Heine to his countrymen: Above all, no emphasis! For now muſt he run the gamut of fearful apprehension—from the firſt shade of anxiety to the complete agony. Slowly the hat begins to decline over one ear . . . O polish'd perturbation! silken care! Never once does the Mr. Griffiths, whom I take to be senior, descend to gross fooling; the quandary is from real life. So a civic worthy who has picked up the covering of a lesser brain. Coquelin's burgess was not more amusing, nor was the key of presentation greatly different. When, later, the brothers became a corporate horse of pantomime variety, they ſtill kept in touch with the world of intelleċt. And here, surely, is the essence of supreme clowning, that it shall derive, originally, from the brain.

The next turn plunged us into the more dismal traditions of the British music-hall. To wreſt from the combined arts of music, coſtume, scene-painting, and the dance such utter joylessness as that prosecuted by the Palace Girls muſt have taxed the utmoſt genius of Mr. John Tiller. Doubtless these young people have talent and to spare; they but do as they are bidden. Nevertheless, I do not remember ever having seen dancers subjugated to such charmless beheſts. The interval was filled with an orcheſtral rehearsal of Sir Harry Lauder's familiar choruses. All around me was a tremor of anticipation. And then the curtain drew up to disclose, not Sir Harry, but an American-Indian Princess, defined on the programme as a *prima donna.* This lady's native wood-notes wild were, one felt, inopportune. She should have sung herebefore. When, finally, her top F had trailed away, there was a gladsome ruſtle. The back-cloth now drew up to show a

Another Essay on the Comic Spirit

vacant stage, and the house settled down for the little man.

Let it be said at once that there is nothing cringing about Lauder. He has the great artist's overweening conceit of himself. He emerges from the wings like the sun from base clouds. He irradiates his world, flattering stalls and gallery with sovereign eye. That a creature like ourselves should glow with such intensity of self-appreciation warms the cockles of the most sceptical heart. Here is one who tastes life to the full, and insists upon our tasting it too. He gives of his superfluity, willy-nilly, like a cup that runs over. His first item is all about a Clydeside sumph and his mistress, Bella the Belle of Dunoon. Lauder makes his lover hardly human. With his rude thatch, squat figure, dependent arms and warped legs, he recalls ancestral boughs. The actor insists wilfully upon this, executing between the verses a jocund step in parody of our father, the ape. It is not until the next song that you size up the artistry of the man. It is a different Lauder who, in the garb of an old salt, puts on the tenderest humanity. The verse is pure doggerel, the tune reminiscent of Mr. Chevalier's " My Old Dutch." Harmony is non-existent. Yet such is the intensity of the emotion conveyed that the whole house, simple and hypercritical alike, fall a-singing:

" There is somebody wai-ai-ting for me
In an old cabin down by the sea,
In the land where I wish I could be
There is somebody wai-ai-ting for me-e-e,
There is somebody wai-ai-ting for me."

Another Essay on the Comic Spirit

The composition is all Sir Harry's own, and I am to admit that it would seem to be the singer's proper, unsimulated emotion which produces the spontaneous and magical effect. And yet the man's an actor. Shade of Diderot and his accursed paradox!

Lamb was wrong when he said that the school of Munden began, *and must end*, with himself. Lauder is in the direct line of Munden. Can any man " wonder," like Lauder ? Can any man " see ghosts," like him, or "fight with his own shadow," as he does? "She'll be full of surprises, In the morning when she rises, To hear I'm in the town," he sings, and as at the word " surprises " he drops his voice to a whisper, Lauder conjures up a poet's vision of first rapture. So Lucy thinking on Richard Feverel. " She laid on my waistcoat, close to my heart," contains the core of " Hang there like fruit, my soul, Till the tree die! " There is a deeper wonder here, surely, than the older actor possessed, or so we must believe. Mundenish in its quiddity is the picture of Doughie the baker, ruminating on the jealousy of his spouse. Doughie describes the two houses and the narrow passage between them as graphically as you would want to describe them to a child. He makes you see the two abodes as they were the painted arks of twin Noahs. The baker was coming home to his tea just as his neighbour, Mrs. McCulloch, emerged upon an errand. They met in the passage " like two trams." " Mind ye," says Doughie with superb, irrelevant insistence, " I canna tell ye what Mrs. McCulloch was going oot for! " The whole of this patter is crowded with particularities which give it credibility. Old favourites followed, and then Sir Harry showed us that

89

doubling of the artist which, on the stage, is least pleasing. He gave an unaccompanied, maudlin song, and a little homily on the blessings of peace.

It must not be supposed that Lauder does not calculate his effects. He does. Each verse is more elaborate than the preceding one, so that the result is both cumulative and culminative. The actor has an exceedingly fine feeling for character. Soldier, sailor, yokel, God's innocent are all to their several manners born. They are true to nature, yet transfigured. Even Doughie, the loutish baker, his face covered with flour, his brow bound with a ragged bonnet, wears about him something elfin, something of Pierrot. Once or twice the daft fellow will cock a malignant eye, and in such a moment the great actor is revealed. Lauder can make a face of horror like the mask of Irving's Dante, confronted with the starving Ugolino. These qualities of pathos and tragedy, like the wistfulness of Chaplin, are not what the generality look for. To them Lauder is a figure of pure fun, with a modicum of sentimental alloy. They love that description of bonnie Wee Jean with her velvet arms round her father's neck, but they adore still more that rueful " But she's got ma nose and ear-r-r-s! " Here again the comic idea is given an ingenious twist. The gist of it is not the superimposing of absurdity upon plain sense, but the discovery of the rational in lunatic or sentimental disguise. When all is said and done the man remains an evangelist whose tidings are of pure Celtic joy.

Another Essay on the Comic Spirit

Continually one hears expressions of regret at the passing of the music-hall. The Palladium has gone over to Revue, the Palace to " the pictures "; either betrayal, apparently, contents the Empire. Even the Euston has fallen, and into aestheticism's very maw. This gives me for Mr. Nigel Playfair that tempered animosity which one feels for the friend who would protect you, willy-nilly, against your lower self, who would bar the way to a pleasant, familiar vice. An enterprise so single in pursuit of pleasure as the music-hall, so avowedly free from moral implications, cannot, the Puritans tell us, be contained within a more polite category. These good people fail to realize that vice and virtue have one thing in common: repress them in one place and they break out in another. Were I to attempt a parallel between this continual chivvying of the music-hall and the harassing of the early churches, I should want to make one point very clear. This point is that persecution, although admittedly the most favourable of soils, is still not more than the mould round the roots of the plant which, if it is to flourish, must contain within itself the vital seeds. Sects and denominations have prospered in the face of persecution simply because there was a genuine demand for their creeds. The music-hall managers have sought to do away with the music-hall programme in the belief that there is no further demand for it. They are wrong. People still want that programme, and will, I submit, continue to want it whenever it is as good as that presented at the Victoria Palace.

All juggling is beautiful, though different performers belong to different orders in beauty. Rastelli, making

Another Essay on the Comic Spirit

of that immemorial trinity of the juggler, his cigar, gloves, and umbrella, a Catherine wheel of beauty, brings to the mind something of the sculptor's sense of rhythm. Mr. Bert Elliott, with his "Topsy-Turvy Toppers," does not soar so high, content with bringing off the feat announced and careless of the finer shades. He throws his three top hats into the air, catching each one on his head in turn so that it executes between forehead and cranium a little dance like that of a spun coin returning to a state of rest. There is a future here for these discarded insignia; our old bonnets are put to their right use, the juggler's head. Rastelli would have made of this trick a glossy symbol of the eighteen nineties; Mr. Elliott declines upon the beauty of efficiency. His technical mastery is, we may think, of the same order as Mr. Mark Hambourg's; none could have played these variations on a theme of top hats more accurately or with a more surpassing swiftness.

The next turn takes us into high life. It is called "Symphonia. A Combination of Instrumental and Vocal Harmony." The curtain rises to disclose a magnificent interior modelled on the Socialist conception of the home life of the idle rich. Disposed about a saloon, of which the spaciousness is accentuated by a grand piano and some standard palms, an obvious baronet and his three daughters take their after-dinner ease. They are all in evening dress. The eldest daughter presides at the piano, the next in staidness nurses her 'cello, the youngest and most frolicsome cuddles a violin. These young ladies care little, apparently, for music in which they can all join, say the simpler Beethoven trios, preferring to entertain papa with soli of

incredible virtuosity. She who plays the violin leads off
with a piece of dull persistence, a " Perpetuum Mobile,"
which I cannot assign to any known composer. This
itch for discovery must run in the blood, since presently
the 'cellist takes up the search with something I assign
to Popper. And now that other Poppa, the head of the
household, intervenes. The widower—for such, alas!
I take the Baronet to be—clears his throat, the lights are
lowered, and he plunges into the thick of his ballad.
It is not an old song and it is not a new one; it impales
us on the horns of the old Spencerian dilemma of the
created or the self-created universe. We cannot imagine
the time when either the music or the words were not.
It is, perhaps, a lawful conception that in the beginning
both were and rushed together, sentimental oxygen and
hydrogen, to form the water of our tears. I may
reproduce here only the words, the music you must
deduce; it is inevitable, and follows the law of mass
emotion:

" There's the road that is rough and stony,
    And it's uphill night and day;
No stile to rest a little while,
    It's a tough road all the way.
There's the road that is all sunshiny,
    It's the road we love to roam,
But the road that leads [*pause*] to Heaven all the while
    Is the road to Home, Sweet Home."

This is received with the most rapturous acclaim,
and really I like it quite as well as Mascagni's Inter-
mezzo, the opening phrase of which is softly warbled

Another Essay on the Comic Spirit

behind the drawing-room's *portière*. And then a fourth, and favourite daughter appears. The Baronet strikes the attitude which Orchardson has laid down for widowers' guidance, and we know that we are listening to her mother's voice. A hush falls upon the house, and I shall not quarrel with you if you say that this Italian treacle, too cloying for any palate of refinement, is yet healthier than the stupefying liquor distilled by the American negro from the gum of his native Jazz tree. The velvet curtains fall and the Baronet's musical evening is at an end.

Mr. Nelson Keys, who follows, is an interloper from a world of which the perceptions are alleged to be finer. This actor possesses the gift which has been lost to us since little Robson; he has the secret of that art of travesty which heightens the emotion of the thing travestied. His portrait of senility succumbing to the Jazz is both ludicrous and terrible; this figure of old age dancing to the grave might have come straight out of an old-fashioned morality. I am tempted to say that this little inch is worth the entire canvases of some more consequential actors. Mr. Keys lets you see the world on a thumb-nail. The sublime of intellectual fooling is reached with his Cook's guide, rapturously seized at the moment of shepherding a party through Trafalgar Square, " a favourite resort of those so wittily described as the working classes." Tears of mirth stream down our faces as we watch the vagaries of that ragged moustache, and listen to that voice now booming like Big Ben when a strong wind blows up the river, now echoing the hollow wash of the tide receding from Fingal's Cave. An extravagant image ? Mr. Keys is an extravagantly

Another Essay on the Comic Spirit

funny actor. On an entirely different plane is Mr.
George Bass, who describes himself as " The Popular
Comedian." " Popular " is entirely just; the people
love him. " I like your socks, George," says the con-
ductor. " Them's not socks," George replies, pulling
up his trousers to show ankles encased in circlets of
scarlet wool. " Them's mittens! " The quality of the
fun here is what the French call *tordant*; the audience
literally twists itself for joy. Mr. Bass is of Formby's
school, the apparent simpleton who is " all there."
With solemnity he declaims:

> " For East is East and West is West,
> Though the fact seems hardly relevant; "

The audience holds breath at the last portentous
word, and needs it all for the immense guffaw released
by the concluding

> " Yet anybody knows you can milk a cow,
> But you can't mess about with an elephant."

Let me add that the programme also contains Miss
Ella Shields, straight as a ramrod in her policeman's
and naval officer's uniforms, some trick-cyclists and
other tumblers. How, then, with all this actual joy and
entire absence of tedium, should people not want the
music-hall ? I want it and shall go on wanting it,
Baronet and all.

95

Mary Queen of Drinkwater

Mary Stuart, by John Drinkwater. Everyman Theatre.

BAD HISTORICAL PLAYS ARE OF two kinds—those which go over familiar ground, and those which break the improbable new. The first bore us with a recital which Hume or Macaulay has accomplished more succinctly; the second do violence to our sense of truth. Good historical plays are of one kind only; they are those which unveil the mind of the historian and reveal not Henry the Fifth but Shakespeare, not Caesar but Mr. George Bernard Shaw. Playwrights like W. G. Wills and Sheridan Knowles were precluded by nature from writing good historical plays; they had no mind to disclose. Or if they had, it was only a very little one, about the size, say of that of the Rev. Mr. Collins. That egregious insect and Lady Catherine would, one feels sure, have been in essential agreement about Wills's " mouthing patriot with the itching palm," though inclining, perhaps, to a nicer conveyance of the sentiment. When Wills is not revealing his lack of wit he is the dullest of truth-tellers. How, at the Ambassadors Theatre, about half-way through the revival of Charles the First, did I not wish that another had been called in to finish it, Münchausen or de Rougemont! Then might we have had Cromwell's head on a pole, which would have been better fun than Wills's exposition of that Great Man's mentality and, between you and me, quite as good history. Not to beat about the bush, such plays are utter rubbish. " Her gossip was to come hot-foot i' the morn." It is a pity that Wills's gossip did not go hot-foot at any hour of the day and call attention to the waste-paper basket. I do not believe that even Mr. Dick would have sat this piece out twice.

And yet, when Irving played it, the piece did not sound such fustian. The great actor had the power of making melodrama seem not real, but noble. In the mind's eye I see him turn that awful face to deliver the old rebuke to Ireton, " Who is this rude gentleman ? " After the word " this " there was a pause. The old man would raise his eyebrows and then, with hooded malevolence like Satan's before the Fall, bring out the next word as though it were Heaven's own blasting charge. Another and a shorter pause, a lesser lift of the eyebrows, and the word " gentleman " would obliterate the demon and restore the saint. When, to Moray, Irving delivered himself of that nonsense about Judas Iscariot, it sounded like the Angel of Compassion. " Judas had eyes like thine "—an ineffable little gulp here—" of tender blue." And the house would instantly dissolve in tears.

Mr. Drinkwater's mind is as fine as Wills's was commonplace. It is unfortunate, however, that he cannot resist whitewash. As soon as his eye lights upon an historical figure it is filled with the gleam proper to the blanching of sepulchres. " Here's a great man; let's whitewash him " is the unspoken word. " Here's Cromwell; we must have a big bucket for him! Abraham Lincoln ? Well, another little coat won't do

97

him any harm. Here's Mary Stuart; let's make her into a Lady Jane Grey." Mr. Drinkwater is a dab hand with the brush.

Against this may be set the view that a theatre is not a place of trial, that the business of the dramatist is to sift the evidence for himself and give the court his summing-up. No character in history has been more debated than Mary's. Was she murderess as well as wanton? If she was not, then her enemies showed the utmost ingenuity in foisting the twofold reputation upon her. Buchanan writes:

> Herself goes to Glasgow; she pretends the cause of her journey to be to see the King alive, whose death she had continually gaped for the month before. But what was indeed the true cause of that journey, every man may plainly perceive by her letters to Bothwell. Being now out of care of her son, whom she had in her own ward, bending herself to the slaughter of her husband, to Glasgow she goes, accompanied with the Hamiltons, and other the King's natural enemies.
>
> Bothwell, as it was between them before accorded, provides all things ready that were needful to accomplish the heinous act; First of all, a house, not commodious for a sick man, nor comely for a King, for it was both riven and ruinous, and had stood empty without any dweller for divers years before, in a place of small resort, between old falling walls of two kirks, near a few almshouses for poor beggars. And that no commodious means for committing that mischief might be wanting, there is a postern door in the Town

Wall, hard by the house, whereby they might easily pass away into the fields. . . .

When all things were ready prepared for performing this cruel fact . . . the Queen, for manners' sake, after supper, goes up to the King's lodging. There being determined to show him all the tokens of reconciled good will, she spent certain hours in his company, with countenance and talk much more familiar than she had used in six or seven months before. At the coming in of Paris, she broke off her talk and prepared to depart. This Paris was a young man born in France, and had lived certain years in the houses of Bothwell and Seton, and afterwards with the Queen. Whereas the other keys of that lodging were in custody of the King's servants, Paris, by feigning certain fond and slender causes, had in keeping the keys which Bothwell kept back, of the back gate and the postern. He was in special trust with Bothwell and the Queen, touching their secret affairs. His coming (as it was before agreed among them) was a watchword that all was ready for the matter. As soon as the Queen saw him, she rose up immediately, and feigning another cause to depart, she said, " Alas! I have much offended toward Sebastian this day, that I came not in a mask to his marriage." This Sebastian was an Avernois (Auvergnois), a man in great favour with the Queen, for his cunning in music, and his merry jesting, and was married the same day. The King thus left, in manner, alone, in a desolate place, the Queen departs, accompanied with the Earls of Argyle, Huntly, and Cassilis, that attended upon her. After that she was come into her chamber, after

midnight, she was in long talk with Bothwell, none
being present but the captain of her guard. And
when he also withdrew himself, Bothwell was there
left alone, without other company, and shortly after
retired into his own chamber. He changed his
apparel, because he would be unknown of such as met
him, and put on a loose cloak, such as the Swart-
rytters* wear, and so went forward through the watch
to execute his intended traitorous fact. The whole
order of the doing thereof may be easily understood
by their confessions who were put to death for it.

Bothwell, after the deed was ended that he went for,
returned, and as if he had been ignorant of all that was
done, he gat him to bed. The Queen, in the meantime, in great expectation of the success, how finely
she played her part (as she thought) it is marvell to
tell; for she not once stirred at the noise of the fall
of the house, which shook the whole town, nor at the
fearful outcries that followed, and confused cries of
the people (for I think there happened her not any
new thing unlooked for) till Bothwell, feigning himself afraid, rose again out of his bed, and came to her
with the Earls of Argyle, Huntly, and Athole, and
with the wives of the Earls of Mar and Athole, and
with the Secretary. There, while the monstrous
chance was in telling, while every one wondered at the
thing, that the King's lodging was even from the
very foundation blown up in the air, and the King
himself slain; in this amazedness and confused fear
of all sorts of persons, only that same heroical heart
of the Queen maintained itself, so far from casting

* German. Black Riders, or heavy cavalry.

herself down into base lamentations and tears, unbeseeming the royal name, blood, and estate, that she matched, or rather far surmounted all credit of the constancy of any in former times. This also proceeded of the same nobility of courage, that she sent out the most part of them that were then about her, to inquire out the manner of the doing, and commanded the soldiers that watched to follow, and she herself settled her to rest, with a countenance so quiet, and mind so untroubled, that she sweetly slept till the next day at noon. But lest she should appear void of all naturalness at the death of her husband, by little and little, at length she kept her close, and proclaimed a mourning not long to endure.

But these, it is contended, were the most devilishly skilful forgeries. That Mary should sleep is not significant; she slept as soundly the night before her execution.

Consider the contents of one of these alleged letters to Bothwell. Guzman de Silva, the Spanish Ambassador, writes to Philip II, on 2nd August, 1567:

> The Earl of Murray went to Scotland on the last day of July. . . . I visited him. . . . He repeated how displeased he was at the action of the lords in taking the Queen. . . . I said that her confessor had told me that as regarded the King's murder she had no knowledge whatever of it, and had been greatly grieved thereat. . . . He opened out somewhat, saying that my good will towards him prompted him to tell me something that he had not

even told this Queen (Elizabeth), although she had
given him many remote hints upon the subject.
This was that he considered it very difficult to
arrange matters, as it was certain that the Queen had
been cognisant of the murder of her husband, and he,
Murray, was greatly grieved thereat. This had been
proved beyond doubt by a letter which the Queen
had written to Bothwell, containing three sheets of
paper, written with her own hand, and signed by her,
in which she says in subſtance that he is not to delay
putting into execution that which he had arranged,
because her husband used such fair words to deceive
her and bring her round that she might be moved
by them if the other thing were not done quickly.
She said that she herself would go and fetch him, and
would stop at a house on the road, where she would
try to give him a draught, but if this could not be
done, she would put him in the house where the
explosion was arranged for the night upon which one
of her servants was to be married. He, Bothwell,
was to try to get rid of his wife either by putting her
away or by poisoning her, since he knew that she, the
Queen, had risked all for him, her honour, her kingdom, her wealth, and her God, contenting herself
with his person alone. Besides this she had done an
extraordinary and unexampled thing on the night of
the murder in giving her husband a ring, petting and
fondling him after plotting his murder, and this had
been the worſt thing in connection with it. Murray
said he had heard about the letter from a man who had
read it, and the reſt was notorious. . . . He says
he will do his beſt for her. I am more inclined to

believe that he will do it for himself if he finds a
chance, as he is a Scotchman, and a heretic. . . .

But, again, we muſt consider that all this is but hear-
say. " Murray said he had heard about the letter from
a man who had read it, and the reſt was notorious."
Professor Rait sums up the case for and againſt Mary
with the moſt admirable discretion:

> What part on this crowded ſtage did Mary play ?
> If she was bad, she was a woman dangerous as few
> women have been dangerous: clever enough to hide
> her cleverness: concealing deep-laid plots under a
> gay prattle of conversation and an artless correspond-
> ence adorned with platitude and copy-book maxims:
> playing with life and death with the innocence of a
> child: a woman magical with an evil magic: employ-
> ing a nature richly dowered with charm solely for the
> gratification of the luſts of the flesh. If she was good,
> she was a woman not remarkable for ſtrong intelleƈtual
> power; but possessed of a personality almoſt unique
> in hiſtory, and a winning grace that few were ſtrong
> enough to resiſt: a womanly woman, desirous of
> taking life as lightly as might be: truſting implicitly
> till she found herself deceived, and ever afterwards
> suspicious: kindly and generous, but capable of a
> feminine bitterness, the gratification of which coſt
> her much: maintaining always, and in all circum-
> ſtances, as one of those who knew her said, " that
> enchantment wherewith men are bewitched."

Forewarned, in the matter of hiſtorical plays, is not
necessarily forearmed. My head buzzing with these

discrepant views about Mary, it was a little disconcerting to have to swallow a sentimentalist of the purest rose-pink and *bleu tendre*. This Mary of Mr. Drinkwater's turned out to be a woman magical with platitude and copy-book maxims. But first there was the young gentleman in the dinner-jacket.

They do things with a praiseworthy solemnity at the Everyman Theatre. To begin with the house is plunged into utter darkness, thus dousing the glim of any lingering levity. Our faces and our minds composed, there ensues a grinding which might be the mills of God, but is, in reality, only the winch which raises the curtain. This having functioned, the morality begins. I have laboured the little idiosyncrasies proper to this theatre because they provide me with an image for the opening of *Mary Stuart*, which does not get under way without much straining at the windlass. The anchor weighed, we perceive not Mary nor any of her lovers, but a young gentleman fingering his dress-tie and bemoaning his inability to satisfy his wife's capacity for spiritual affection. Now since the function of a good historical play is to tell us about the mind of the writer, and since Mr. Drinkwater is an acknowledged master of the historical play, we ought to enter with zest into the author's thesis that a young woman who has married an unimaginative stockbroker is morally entitled to find livelier paramours among his friends. In Mr. Drinkwater's view a man who talks about his " honour " is a scoundrel. " History seethes with the error (the aforesaid honour), society is drenched with it." Well, this may be so, and since Mr. H. O. Nicholson, who enunciated the strange philosophy, in endeavouring to follow

Mary Queen of Drinkwater

the stage-direction that he should look like Charles the First in imaginary dotage succeeded in resembling M. Anatole France in his very green old age, I was perfectly inclined to put the old foolish beliefs on one side and follow the new prophet. Only, Mr. Drinkwater, it should have been upon some other occasion; we were assembled to hear the old tale of Mary Queen of Scots. At this point that hussy walked in through the window and told the young gentleman that her own life would make him see his wife's wantonness in a proper and a virtuous light. " Boy, I can tell you everything," is all she said, but the above was what she meant. Another plunge into darkness, more ominous creaking, and the curtain went up on Holyrood.

Mary is perfectly candid with herself. If she could have read thirty years ahead she would have applied to her own person Enobarbus's *mot* about another queen, " Her passions are made of nothing but the finest part of pure love." Her own way of putting it is that not Rizzio, not Darnley, and not Bothwell knew how to find " this Mary's best magnificence of the great lover's mind." And yet one feels that this Mary, this gormandizer whom our author makes to appear so fastidious and so frail, would have made certain spiritual reservations in the matter of " pure love," that she would not have accepted unmodified the old soldier's sense of pure amativeness. Mary has an exquisite passage in which she pleads that in addition to her restless fires she has other longings—" to see strong children about me, to play with an easy festival mind, to walk the evenings at peace." Now this sounds innocent and is beautifully put, yet it is also exactly what a guilty and jaded Mary would have said. Courtesans before Dumas *fils* have sighed for *pureté, campagne*, and an *amant de cœur*. It is typical of Mr. Drinkwater's innocence that he should make this spiritually " nice " Mary fall into the idiom of the sentimental *cocotte*. The Queen has been described as a " brave spirit " who was also " dastard and dupe." Of her bravery none doubts, nor are her dastardly qualities seriously questioned. The dramatist, it seems to me, has canonized the dupe. In short, his imaginary portrait won't quite do. It is like one of those marble busts, popular with Victorian sculptors, which tapered to the waist and came to no legs. One feels that though the writer makes Mary prate of passion, it is to be deemed passion in the abstract. He would, we feel, be shocked at the idea that the Queen ever took her *gigolo* to bed.

In the matter of the murder of Darnley, Mr. Drinkwater muddled me completely. Bothwell was " wise " to it, Mary apparently not. She seemed to me to deserve Lady Macbeth's contempt, so very much was she the cat i' the adage. Stripped of her poetry, she seemed—dare I say it?—to be just the least little bit of a fool. Mary completely justified, for me, the historian who described her as being " of such dastardly imbecility, heartless irresolution, and brainless inconsistency as to dispose of her claim to intelligence and courage." But I doubt if such was the dramatist's intention. By any other name the piece is one of singular beauty.

Miss Laura Cowie's performance was intelligent and painstaking, and conveyed a flower-like delicacy of mind. But within that Queen's breast, placid as Rydal Water on summer eves, were no hidden storms. It is curious that Miss Cowie's profile should so strongly resemble Réjane's. This, again, is against her, for we look to see the nostrils quiver like those of a horse, to watch the fire leap to the eyes and the face grow grey with passion. The English actress has none of this, only a childlike purity and wistfulness. The part calls for a greater thrust and urgency of beauty than she at present possesses. It is cut to the measure of Mrs. Patrick Campbell, and I should have thought that that lady would have gone down on her knees to Mr. Drinkwater and begged once more to play the artist.

A Sermon to Communists

Wat Tyler, by Halcott Glover. "Old Vic."

WHEN I READ MR. HALCOTT Glover's *Wat Tyler* I believed it to be the finest English play of the last hundred years. A performance at the "Old Vic" has left me in doubt as to whether it is a work for the stage at all. In the theatre the struggle between Wat, the man of action, and Ball, the man of dreams, was neither as emotional nor as thought-compelling as, in the law-courts, the recent duel between Mr. William Watson and the Duke of Northumberland. Critics have complained that Mr. Glover makes them think of his four-teenth-century hero in terms of Mr. Smillie and Mr. Thomas. I, thinking of him in terms of Mr. Watson, do not make this complaint. It seems to me that Mr. Glover does better to throw back into the past the burn-ing matters of the hour than to write historical drama void of modern interest. Let me say here that I hold no brief for Mr. Watson, that I believe the wreck of civilization to be encompassed in his views. But inas-much as I conceive them to be sincere and their enun-ciator a visionary, so do I hear again the voice of John Ball. Not Communism, but the Communist would ruin us all. Not the seers of visions, but those who would put them into practice bring the world about their ears.

A Sermon to Communists

The play opens with the putting into the stocks of a vagabond from whose belt they have taken a hammer, with village rumours of the slaying of a tax-gatherer by the hammer, with a discussion between the King's Commissioner and the people of the Poll Tax and the Statute of Labour. The people choose a man of their own, one Jack Straw, to speak for them. (Is not this the Trades Union way to-day?) Straw asks whether he and his kind made the wars for which they are to be taxed. The Commissioner replies that the King's enemies made the wars and that the people, as loyal subjects, went overseas to defend their liberties. "There is nothing new in this." Nor yet anything old. Mr. Watson's friends are agog with it to-day. Straw asks for a leader, and the man in the stocks, Wat Tyler, offers himself. He rescues Ball from prison and sets him at the head of the rebellion. Tyler has faith in kingliness and believes that the King, if he can but get to him, will redress his grievances. A few broken heads, a little blood-letting, but no radical upheaval. Ball, however, finds virtue not in kingship, but in low estate. It is enough for him if a man have nothing. "When I have closed the dying eyes of wretches and of harlots I have seen shining therein the souls of the valiant, the great spirits whose lot was fell: who, dying, went back to God honourable as soldiers full of wounds." He envisages his death and a thousand generations' deaths. "Freedom shall come, if not in my day, then in some far age or country." He is one of those uncommon men who bring ruin upon common enterprises. He drinks the people's cause and urges the mob to holy war; it returns drunk with pillage and with slaughter. To Ball, too late, comes the

109

perception that he has propped men above earth and that the very spirituality of his support was its weakness. He passes beyond our ken, a man down whose side run water and blood. The play ends with the bringing in of Tyler's body. In reading I could very well understand why Mr. Glover omitted the actual death-scene. The issue is not romantic, but fundamental; not of men, but of principles. " Wat Tyler and John Ball destroy each other, to the end of time. Only Hodge remains."

The overthrow of the idealist by his ideal is an old note of tragedy and one that should be sounded again to-day. Communism were unassailable if its instruments were not flesh and blood. Communism is a Holy Grail; its followers are too often those who seek out Beauty to destroy it. Communism would lift up the heads of the people; they are its disciples who go about with pikes seeking to elevate the heads of the rich. Communism's device may run: " Not as devils, with hideous joy, but as clean men, striking no blow that can be spared." Yet we behold Russia. These high priests look before, but not after.

> " Sow seed—but let no tyrant reap;
> Find wealth—but let no impostor heap;
> Weave robes—let not the idle wear;
> Forge arms—in your defence to bear "

is all very well. Yet we may be sure that Shelley, arrested for incitement to murder, would have stressed the meaning of the last five words. So your Hyde Park orator pleads too late that his threat to hang a Cabinet Minister indicated a purely Pickwickian process of dependence. Gandhi, Lenin, and Trotsky and, for all

we know, Mr. Watson, bethink themselves after the
event. Yet I must believe all revolutionaries to be not
self-seeking butchers but seers before their time. The
world shrinks intolerably else.

Mr. Glover's great piece of philosophy failed to move
me in the theatre. Yet the words fell with dignity upon
the ear; they were of the soil of English speech. The
scenery, costing, I suppose, a ten-pound note, was
exquisite. I have rarely seen anything more satisfying
than that brown sail, glimpsed over the parapet of
London Bridge, against the turquoise of the night and
the first flushings of the dawn. Only the " ploughman-
cloth," which was lowered between each scene, was not
quite effective. Intended to be unlovely, humorous,
like the man with the spade in Ford Madox Brown's
" Work," it was too much like a music-hall personification by Mr. Jay Laurier. The difficulty with the play,
I must think, is the unwillingness of the stage to go
outside its proper medium. Reading, you sent your
mind questing after remembrances of the soil, rich
fields and blessed rain. Listening, you were conscious
only that these were bad actors. Why, you asked
fretfully, would Tyler persistently stress all the unimportant words ? Why did he look like that woodcut of a
king—probably Henry II—which adorns all childish
history books, a foolish figure wearing a crown, a night-
gown to his feet, and an insipid beard ? Why did he
make no figurative use of the cross from the steps of
which he addresses the crowd ? One felt that there was
no man here. John Ball, too, was but a shell. Mr.
Ernest Milton gave him, rightly, the look of something
uncoffined. But when he spoke you were conscious of

the spirit of rhetoric rather than the body of conviction. He should have torn your heart with human pity, yet given you glimpses of the Judgment Seat. The last speech was, however, finely done. The dungeon scene was too dark; the voice and intonations of this actor hardly bear the fierce beat of almost total night.

The New Immorality

I Serve, by Roland Pertwee. Kingsway Theatre.

SOME PEOPLE HAVE AN ANNOYING habit of saying to one: " Of course I read your notice. Tell me, what did you *really* think of the play ? " And this after one has spent many anxious hours in getting on to paper one's exact shade of meaning. Others, who do not read one, are necessarily less subtle, but not less inquisitive. " I suppose you've seen ' Singing in the Wilderness ' ? " they say, with a fine off-hand assumption. " At the Omar Theatre, isn't it ? " I probably counter, filling the gap and giving back the *réplique*. " Of course," they go on, somewhat guiltily, " it's awful nonsense, but we rather liked it." The trouble with these good people is that they use "but" when they mean " and therefore." They are ashamed to confess that a play is rubbish, and that they enjoy it just because it is rubbish. (There is, of course, a still happier class which likes the bad without knowing it to be bad. Where ignorance is bliss, 'tis folly to be critical.)

I am inclined to blame the dramatic critics for what, in these playgoers, is really moral cowardice. They will insist upon applying to the theatre the specious apothegm that we needs must love the highest when we see it. Inversely they reason that whatever the public loves to see in its largest numbers must in its view be

the highest art. Whereupon they bludgeon the poor
dears for being stupid, instead of gently chiding them
for being naughty. If only the critics would realize
that a great part of the public has only to glimpse the
lowest to fall in love with it. An eminent surgeon,
who is also something of a philosopher and a dab hand
at the problems of cognition, once told me that his only
reading matter consisted of the latest surgical treatise
and, after dinner, Emanuel Kant (in the original, I
wormed out of him) and the racing novels of Nat Gould.
He disliked indifferently Shakespeare and Dickens,
Jane Austen and Pett Ridge; these took him back to
life, whereas what he sought was escape. He never
went to the theatre; no drama, he explained, was bad
enough for him. I instance my friend as a typical
member of the great public, who, untypically, was
honest with himself and with me. Honesty by itself,
however, does not constitute a critic, and I should
hesitate to recommend this guileless philosopher for a
Chair of Letters. Willy-nilly the critic must don the
Arthurian mantle; the whole reason for his existence
lies in his acceptance of that old tag which poor Guine-
vere undoubtedly pinched from her lord. Should I,
a trifle loosely, say of Mr. Roland Pertwee's *I Serve*,
at the Kingsway Theatre, that it was rubbish, *but* that I
enjoyed it very much, I really mean that I found something to like in it which was very far from rubbish.

I had not intended to go to the play that afternoon.
Passing the Kingsway Theatre one day, the thought
came into my head that it might be a refreshing experience to visit a show non-professionally, " for fun " as it
were. So in I went, to the sparsely-filled pit. (It is good

The New Immorality

from time to time to mingle with human beings instead of first-nighters.) I had no programme and knew nothing of play or cast. A forebodingly comic plumber was mending a grate, while a maidservant—arch and coy, I felt sure, as soon as she should turn round—was "answering the door" up-stage. (I have a rooted dislike to plays which begin like this.) Suddenly my heart gave a great leap; I recognized that the actress was Miss Edith Evans. From that moment this exquisite player held not only me but all that handful of an audience—the stalls, alas! were thin too—in thrall as poignant as that in which, years ago, Mr. George Moore held us with *Esther Waters*. That novel was a masterpiece; this little play was to tremble too often on the brink of absurdity. Yet there was also to be found in it that which was both moving and true. The motive of the piece is illegitimacy; the thesis that it is the moral duty of the father to acknowledge his offspring. *Reconnaître ses enfants* is a legal term in France. To this end it is supposed that a law has been passed in this country, whereby a father may, by marriage at any time, legitimize his natural child. The mother is a maidservant, her child a boy of sixteen. The father is unaware of the boy's existence, his old passion long since dead. He loves Kate's mistress. The maid, in turn, loves the sympathetic, not comic, plumber. But Kate is the most appalling little snob imaginable; she adores, most of all, a "gentleman," and is determined that her boy shall be one. She achieves incredible things, including a mastery of the Latin tongue, that she may fit him for a public school. She teaches him to call her "mater" and, so far as we can gather, conceals the fact that she is a servant. She inherits an unexpected fortune; her mistress loses hers. The two change places, and Kate supports her mistress's lover, who is also Kate's seducer, by giving him a job at three times his proper salary. Her mind is a morass of quasi-gentility, with tufts and tussocks of natural gentleness. Her treatment of her former mistress is adorable; her translation to a new social stratum is dignified, unpretentious, and honest. Yet she hankers ever, for her son's sake, after an engagement; to be announced, poor girl, in the " Morning Post." To this end she employs blackmail —threatening the seducer with loss of his job—and the weak fellow consents to the marriage. We, who realize that the disadvantages of bastardy to the bastard are material and not spiritual, who know that the accident of legitimacy does nothing to make a man virtuous or wise, sober or brave, look on Kate's passion with amazement. The repair of her own " honesty " is never in question; what she is after is her boy's right to the " idea of " gentility. The whole point is that Kate sticks to her unreasoned and unreasonable faith as steadfastly as her betters will stand by a code which they have sounded utterly, that she orders her life by it, and will give up her lover in its behalf. That her outlook appears fantastic to us does not prevent it from being real to her. We look on at the conflict in this uneducated mind very much as an unequivocating Buddhist might survey the doubtings and distractions of a Robert Elsmere—in sympathy, yet without participation. What Western morality is this, which is to rule at the expense of making everybody miserable, and does not even promote the happiness of the boy himself ? He, decent fellow, as

The New Immorality

soon as he learns that his father is a gentleman, goes off to be an engineer. (" Gentleman," in Kate's mind, means a person with an inherited right to wear fine clothes; the word, for her, has only a polite, not moral, significance.) In the course of his engineering the boy is killed, so that Kate and her seducer find their respective happinesses. Our Buddhist would think that, surely, a curious morality which demands the sacrifice of an innocent person to make things comfortable all round. Suppose, too, that a man had two children by different women. Must he marry both ? A thing may be beautiful, said Ruskin, which is yet utter balderdash. *I Serve* is sometimes perilously like nonsense, yet it is full of beauty.

I have always found it difficult to keep my admiration of Miss Edith Evans within reasonable bounds. Her catty old ladies were creations after the heart of Louis Wain; her Cleopatra according to Dryden was a Lely her young woman in *Heartbreak House* a Sargent. Her Kate is the most finished piece of acting on the London stage to-day, perfect both spiritually and in externals, whether as the ultra-ladylike maid, or as the slightly vulgar *châtelaine*. It is the portrait of a great artist who possesses the gift of observation, a fine sense of comedy and the pathos of Mrs. Kendal. The end of the play found the little house in tears, with one exception. I had shed all mine in the earlier acts, in sheer joy at so much beauty and felicity. Mr. Sam Livesey, as the honest plumber, is extraordinarily good. So, too, is Mr. Pertwee himself, as the seducer. He does not pretend that the advent of the son is cataclysmal, or that no man before him has had a natural child.

117

Three Periods

The Second Mrs. Tanqueray, by A. W. Pinero. The
   Playhouse.
Mid-Channel. Royalty Theatre.
The Enchanted Cottage. Duke of York's Theatre.

DEARLY I LOVE THE OLD PLAY. AS
Cayley Drummle would put it, *c'est plus
fort que moi.* I love that delicate snobbery
which, in 1893, saw the world in " our little
parish of St. James's." I love those demoded ethics,
that adventurous jargon. Old memories cluster about
the opening scene. In the corners of the stalls lurk
shades of exquisites, wearing the wraiths of gar-
denias in their button-holes. 'Tis Cayley their one-
time crony who summons them, reckoning, like Elliston's great ghost before him, Lady Orreyed's fish,
cutlet, and pancake as nothing. Once again faded
doctor and shadowy Q.C. help the innocent worldling
over his hurdles in that really lamentable account of the
first Mrs. Tanqueray. Phantom playgoers watch him
gather gusto and phrasing for that ultimate obstacle.
" Paint her portrait, it would symbolize a creature
perfectly patrician; lance a vein of her superbly-
modelled arm, you would get the poorest *vin ordinaire.*"
Will Cayley " negotiate " it ? He does. The ghosts
put lavender palm to lavender palm, and a self-satisfied
shadow gives place to Paula.
   It is pleasant to sit rapt before the young Pinero's

Three Periods

vision of a humanity as magnificently out of drawing as Blake's. What marvellous, overgrown bodies and puny, attenuated heads have these " men and women who can't be imitated! " It is a world of moral security. No Shavian demon whispers that the Aubreys and the Cayleys are anti-social parasites, at once sentimental and gross, passing encumberers of the world; nor insists that in the Paulas we shall see untruthful urns of ever-lasting beauty. The futility of rehabilitation will nowhere be set against the utility of loveliness. The evening, we are confident, will be free of such Greek nonsense. Not yet has the repertory playwright arisen to insist that the poor shall be always with us, even in the theatre. For this occasion, at least, *relâche*. We shall be afflicted by none whose income is less than two thous-and a year, unless it be a servant. Reality will keep her distance. There will be question not of accounting for Paula, but of explaining her away. " How did Alex-ander act ? " somebody asked Wilde after the perform-ance on that May evening thirty years ago. " He didn't; he *behaved*! " was the reply. Paula's dose of poison has nothing to do with a rational despair; it is the last word in decorum. Death ends all things, and, in the last act of a play, puts a convenient stopper on inconvenient questions of morality. The moral of this play may be left till the audience has got home. Are the men to be sure that the Aubreyish indiscretion of marriage will find them out ? Are the women to determine never to " regularize their position " until the man's daughter is safely married ? Both doctrines are dangerous. The dramatist here resembles the lady-novelist who, steering for Scylla and Charybdis, missed both.

Three Periods

Can it be that, in looking for subtleties, we have all these years missed the obvious ? Can it be that young Mr. Pinero meant simply that the Paulas ought not to exist ? Was he merely courtesan-baiting ? The reply is that this particular Paula, in actual life, never did or could exist. She is a legacy from the old Dumasian cant which, crystallized into two sentences, defrayed for fifty years the philosophic cost of plays about these ladies. Dumas, aided and abetted by Desclée, Bernhardt, and a score of others, enveloped the truth in a haze of sentimentality. " On a toujours eu une enfance, quoi que l'on soit devenue " and "Ainsi, quoi qu'elle fasse, la créature tombée ne se relèvera jamais ! " are the two sentences which have caused more facile tears and done more intellectual harm than any other two in the drama of speciousness and gloss. Fallen creatures contract, in real life, the habit of falling on their feet and not requiring to be picked up. That they were once children is axiomatic; the deduction, affected by playwrights, that vice is an external accident and not an inherent development, is a sentimental untruth. Dumas *fils* wrote exquisite rubbish; Sacha Guitry trumpeted the unvarnished truth when he made his little feather-head declare: "Ma mère en était, ma sœur en est, moi j'en suis, que voulez-vous ? " Paula belongs to the days of *La Dame aux Camélias*. Aubrey has the impertinence to tell Paula what she was at Ellean's age, and at the portrait of her alleged innocence, she must needs fall a-weeping on the sofa—" O God ! A few years ago ! " Now this is not truth, but the theatre. Let me, hastily, jot down what I venture to think Paula would really have said, deferring the occasion until after Ardale's arrival. Give me leave to retain the idiom, and utilize the playwright's well-known *penchant* for a story. I imagine Paula restive, and breaking in upon Tanqueray's sermonizing: " I'll tell you what I was at Ellean's age! I was little mother to the women I was to become, Paula Dartry, Paula Ethurst, Paula Ardale, Paula Jarman, Paula Tanqueray, Paula —— whoever the next may be, dear, if you should throw me over. I may have looked as namby-pamby— forgive me—as Ellean, but the resemblance—I assure you—was entirely superficial. Even in those days I realized that to be petted was my vocation. To be-gown and be-jewel us flatters your man's vanity, and the more it costs you the better you're pleased. I got my first lesson in expensiveness when I was a year younger than Ellean. It was at Paillard's, where I was supping with Selwyn Ethurst. At the next table was the most beautiful woman I had then seen, squired by a Frenchman with an impeccable beard. Her eyelashes, said Selwyn, were like the petals of dog-daisies clotted with lamp-black. But if ever I have seen a woman perfectly bored, it was that woman ... I wonder if my eyes have acquired that look since you, I, and Ellean threw out roots in this deadly-lively soil ... From time to time the man rested the tips of his fingers on the plush of the settee, the silk of the woman's dress, the satin of her shoulder. He seemed to be appraising her costliness. We left the restaurant at the same time. As my beauty was being helped into her carriage she dropped her cloak. ' Leave it,' she commanded. ' You can buy me another.' That, Aubrey, was my first lesson in extravagance. You know you like me to like fruit when it's expensive. When I was Ellean's age I was busy acquiring expensive taﬆes, and not waﬆing time dispensing what you call noble thoughts to a parcel of schoolgirls. Now give Ellean her game of bezique and send Ardale to me. I'll manage the reﬆ. Run along, dear, we've had quite enough intelleﬅual honeﬆy for one evening." That, or something like it, is what Paula would have said. The result of such a speech, of course, would have been the withdrawal of the play after the firﬆ performance. Your Englishman is for the tragedy of morals rather than the comedy of manners. Strip edification from your tale of the half-world, and he will have none of it. Public policy demands that the fallen creature shall not rehabilitate herself. Well, Pinero made a fine ﬆage-play out of the old insincerities, old, that is, in a grown-up country like our neighbours'. In England *The Second Mrs. Tanqueray* began as a bombshell and endures as a landmark. With it English drama emerged from the Robertsonian nursery, and took for the firﬆ time since the eighteenth century a man's look at the world. But the view should have been dated "Théâtre du Vaudeville, le 2 février 1852."

The play has the power to make an aﬅress. It made Mrs. Patrick Campbell; it will make Miss Gladys Cooper. I am inclined to think that the younger player feels the part more deeply than her predecessor. She shows more pathos, but has less momentum. Everything that she does at the Playhouse is admirable; at the St. James's that other aﬅress, without need to lift a finger, *was* Paula. This being said, there remains little but praise. The new Paula is blonde, with her hair parted and smoothed to virginal provocation. Her dropped earrings give her the air of Malibran and the

Three Periods

beauties of 1830, and she has, on the sofa, a pose that Manet might have used for the *petit lever* of an Olympe. Say that she is, as Balzac said of Josépha, inexact, capricious, greedy, witty, at times good-natured. You need a gallery of images to fit her. The great outburst in the second act was finely done, although I thought the earlier assumption of impertinence a trifle strained. It verged upon the gutter. Miss Cooper handled the difficult third act very skilfully, being, as was proper, the more moving in her second bout of crying; and her last act was altogether better than Mrs. Campbell's. At the words " You'll see me just as your daughter does now, as all wholesome folks see women like me," the actress raised the very spectre of Retribution. It is a reasoned, conscientious performance of great beauty, and in it Miss Cooper makes her nearest approach to great acting.

There are certain things as to which it seems hardly decent that even the post-war occupants of the stalls should be uninformed. One night during the revival of *The Second Mrs. Tanqueray* my neighbours—obviously a shop-girl and her young gentleman from the motor stores—almost rent the act drop in twain with their excited discussions, not of the new Paula, but as to how the play would end! Unashamed inquiry is better than pretence, or even indifference, and at the Royalty Theatre recently one regretted that there were not a greater number of the ingenuous desirous to know how *Mid-Channel* would end. I counted thirty empty stalls—a state of affairs which should not be. Let me make it clear that there is no question of moral obligation here.

Three Periods

A playhouse is a temple consecrated to the play, and the congregation which assembles with the ulterior motive of improving its mind, manners, or morals, commits an offence against the true spirit of the drama. Those who go to see this play of shipwreck in mid-marriage because it will help them to tide over their own shoals, or because Sir Arthur Pinero is a great name, or even because a pre-war generation deemed the play a good one, do not deserve to enjoy it. The true playgoer goes to see *The School for Scandal* not that he may avoid disparity of age in wedlock, nor because Sheridan is a great name, nor yet because he cares a fig how his great-grandfathers were amused. He goes because he enjoys looking forward to what Joseph will say, and Sir Peter will do when the screen falls.

Mid-Channel is a good play because we want urgently to know what will be said by Ferris and done by Blundell when the lover opens the door behind which Blundell's wife is concealed. It is a very good play because it makes us debate what the characters would or should have done in real life. And it is a supremely good piece of playwriting, because the climax is made to appear not an isolated trick of pretty craftsmanship, but the culminating point in a sequence of inevitable happenings. We do not feel, as in the purely artificial drama, that if the postman had not mislaid the letter the tragedy would not have happened. We feel that even if the petty informer had not blabbed about Zoe her affair with Ferris must have come to light; that if Blundell had not driven his wife into her lover's arms on that particular day he would have done so on the next; that the philanderer's other sweetheart is merely an added

124

complication. This minor intrigue reminds one of those competitions called "Hard Cases," popular in the 'seventies, of which the correct solution depended upon considerations, not of morality, but of good form. And since even Sir Arthur's major intrigues are founded ultimately upon good form, let me standardize them in a typical Hard Case. "First Incident. Mr. A, who is unmarried, has formed a strong, but purely platonic, attachment for Lady B who, confessing to her husband her passion for A, leaves home and writes to inform A of the state of affairs. What should A do? Second Incident. Lord B declares that unless A co-operates in a divorce suit and marries Lady B, he will shoot A. Again, what should A do?" I can think of no play of Pinero of which the excitement does not in the end boil down to the plain question: What is it socially expedient that A should do? In the fourth act of *Mid-Channel* the question is fired at the lover point blank. Ferris is heartily sick of Zoe, and is, moreover, engaged to a pretty girl. What should F do?

When one discusses what Ferris would or should have done, one takes for granted the world which Sir Arthur knows so well, and not some Utopian, harumscarum community. From the " repertory " point of view the inhabitants of this world must be an intolerable crew: they all have too much money; Blundell regards his mistress as possessing no soul to save, but only a bank balance to repair, the moral knot coming neatly asunder when a valedictory cheque is split between two thousand pounds and three; Zoe herself has no concern with anything in Heaven above or the earth beneath save only a good time. " What's the

matter ? " asks Peter Mottram. "Life, dear old chum!"
she whimpers. " Ain't much in it ? " " Dam little! "
It is useless to point out that Zoe's life would have been
" broadened " if she had made a hobby of hemstitching
moral pocket-handkerchiefs.

This is a play about a woman who is unhappy in the
sphere to which, presumably, it has pleased God and not
the repertory playwright to call her. Art may begin at
Hampstead, but let us not pretend that it ends there.
That people eat with knives and forks instead of their
fingers is really no reason why a play should not be made
about them. I confess to an intense longing to see the
stalls filled by people who do not, as the children say,
" sticky " their programmes, and to see elegance
restored on both sides of the curtain. When Jane
Clegg's husband was unfaithful, all poor Jane could do
was to pull a long face till he came home, and a longer
one when he lifted the latch. Now quite between you
and me and the bored policeman at the back of the pit,
a play about Jane isn't frightfully thrilling; it is Henry
Clegg who enchants us. I knew a charwoman once
whose married life was equally pitiful. An unwilling
mediator, I could at best arrange that the husband
should continue in unfaithfulness, but desist from
brutality. The poor woman was satisfied, but I doubt
if I could have made a satisfactory play about her.
Now, if I had been that other mediator, Peter Mottram,
should I have pretended to both sides that each was
guilty of no more than a disregard of appearances ? I
hope not. Should I have urged them to come together
again with an almost imperceptible join like a piece of
china from the best riveters ? I think not. In real life

Three Periods

I should have advised both Zoe and her husband to make a clean breast of it to each other, and fix up some working compromise or seek divorce. And then I should have gone home and written a rattling good play about people who inhabit expensive flats and clip their " g's ", with obsequious valets and the air of being "the right thing." (Hard Case: A has been educated at Eton. What should A do ?) How splendid to write that young sprig's exotic command about the dress-clothes: " Pink lining. Opera. Two pairs of gloves! " One would have written no more that day. It was the fashion at one time to mock at the diction of Sir Arthur's characters. When, for instance, Peter Mottram would assure himself that Blundell knows what he is driving at, he says, airily: " You follow me ? You grasp the poetic allegory ? " It is said that people do not talk like that, but I am not so sure. I think that perhaps Sir Arthur himself may talk like that. On my way to the theatre that evening I read his *obiter dictum* on rejuvenation by monkey glands—" The prospect is alluring." That is Peter to the life, and I am not put off by it. I am, however, a little put off by Zoe's suicide. Consider her position. She has already given up her lover once; she doesn't really care for her husband; *and she has independent means.* Whether we like to admit it or not, more people die of broken income than of broken heart. My charwoman, abandoned of her husband, would have had some excuse for jumping into the river since, presently too old for charing, she must rely upon his three pounds a week. Jane Clegg was in better trim for suicide than Zoe, whose only excuse was that plays at the St. James's Theatre must have a moral ending.

Three Periods

And suicide, on the stage, makes moral all that goes
before. In short, Zoe's situation is really no more than
a Hard Case—What should Z have done? Hard
Cases make bad law, says the jurist, and bad transcrip-
tions from life, says your repertory playwright. But, to
any non-highbrow way of thinking, they make thundering good plays.

Miss Irene Vanbrugh cannot, in the lifetime of
another actress, be considered the greatest of dears, but
she is a dear all the same. One would give her a big hug
for allowing herself to appear positively plain, and so
let Zoe's story tell its own tale. They say that this
actress's technique is old-fashioned. If it is, then
Heaven be thanked! I have not seen a more perfect
piece of acting since, years ago, Réjane made a third-
act entry with her eyes and even nose red with weeping.
One little fault I must urge, that of too many wrong
stresses. Miss Vanbrugh will say, for example, " *He*
needn't have jumped on me before I got the key out of
the lock " with the accent on the " he," and the rest of
the sentence a long diminishing wail. There is no
question of anybody else jumping on her. Mr. Lion,
a very good actor of old men when they may profitably
resemble Pan or some frivolous elderly goat, was not
well suited; he made Peter too proud of his smart
clothes. I would suggest to Miss Janet Eccles that she
cut at least a yard and a half off the streamer attached to
Ethel Pierpoint's hat; it gets in the way of the plot.
Miss Helen Morris's Mrs. Annerly was a clever performance—of the wrong woman. Is it a concession to
the post-war audience that a courtesan must necessarily
wear the air of having been dragged in from the nearest

saloon lounge ? Neither Blundell nor his man would have tolerated the woman for ten minutes. At the Playhouse Lady Orreyed is similarly degraded. Both are mistakes, though well-executed ones.

To whom shall I compare " our foremost playwright " in his latest manner ? Shall I compare him to his earlier day, remembering the round consolation the poet tacks on to his " every fair from fair sometimes declines " ? Nothing it may please this distinguished dramatist to write now can take from him possession of that fair he owns or deprive him of that place in the history of the English theatre which his brilliant craftsmanship has won. Unimpressed to-day by his skin-deep profligates, sentimental harlots, and half-willed creatures of emancipation, we must remember the date of their appearance. Even if Sir Arthur had wanted to tell more than the superficial truth about them, were not Clement Scott and all the other watchdogs of social security ready to bark him out of the acted theatre as they had tried to do with Ibsen ? And Sir Arthur did so desperately want to be acted. Performance was the very breath of his nostrils. Having secured by means of the best farces ever written a hearing and a theatre, he looked round him for passions which should be both safe and reasonably real. Reproached with being no conversationalist, a great French dramatist replied, " *Je ne suis pas moins Corneille!* " Reproached with being no sociologist, Sir Arthur might justly have retorted, " I am not the less Pinero ! And," he might have added, " I am a playwright who is acted! " As we have just seen, in *Mid-*

Channel, he gave the impression that he was impelled to say something outside the theatre and that he sought his beloved boards only to give his thought expression. In this latest play I have the same feeling. And the thought, I venture to say, was not that he could beat another playwright at his own game. Pinero keeps his people in their characters. He does not make a money-lender talk metaphysics, and he probably knows better than his critics how little abstract is his bent. Life, to him as dramatist, has always been an elaborate jig-saw puzzle. Life may not be anything of the sort, but considered in this fashion, it has yielded him brilliant patterns. The impelling notion of the present play is that plain people may be beautiful in each other's eyes. Had this been a novel the characters could safely have remained plain. On the stage they call for physical change, which may only be achieved by fantastic device. And since not even Sir James Barrie can take out a patent in faery, *The Enchanted Cottage* is not an infringement. It is curious that whilst the poetry nearly, or almost nearly, comes off, the jig-saw obstinately refuses to do anything of the sort. Perpend.

Oliver Bashforth is an officer broken in the war. He complains bitterly that he cannot face the women who formerly admired his good looks, that in his set none will devote herself to a cripple. He adds naïvely that he has eight hundred a year. Recalling the shrivelled and twisted spar of human wreckage who, as I passed into the theatre, had offered me chocolates, I wanted to lead this whining hero past the silent Cenotaph and thrust his blind nose into one of those singing posters of St. Dunstan's. I wanted to assemble in the Albert

Three Periods

Hall the women of his class and tell them of that French peasant-girl who, promised to a limbless sufferer, silenced all remonstrances with a steady " *C'est mon homme!* " Mr. Nares, you see, was not helpful. He acted cleverly and sincerely, but I refused to believe him the poltroon of his words. And it was essential that I should so believe him. I do not complain that the dramatist should insist upon an unsympathetic hero; would that there were more of them. I will even, for argument's sake, pretend that Mr. Nares was the cad of Sir Arthur's hypothesis. I will assume, too, that to avoid the ministrations of an unpleasant sister he would in real life carry out his plan of marriage with a plain girl, and tell her to her face that their union will be an act of mutual charity. Here again I am making a concession. To me Miss Laura Cowie was always lovely from the moment she stepped on to the stage. A fourteenth-century painter would have found his ideal Madonna in that vainly imagined frump. Her spirit shone through her. However, I will assume that she was unpleasing, and I will agree to be interested in the blind fellow who could not see that she was another Little Dorrit.

Now comes the fairy part of it. Laura dreams of a gorgeous wedding and a beautiful bride. And lo and behold she *is* beautiful! That is to say she wears a blue velvet dinner-gown and does her hair in such a way that no painter of any century would look at her, whilst Oliver has straightened out. But for the incredibly botched stage-management which follows, the fantasy might, I think, succeed. We are supposed to see the wraiths of former lovers going to their bridal beds. What we actually see is flesh and blood actors turning the stage into an expensive caravanserai of the Italian Lakes during the honeymoon season, with the band discoursing after-dinner romances and *colloques sentimentales*. Sir Frederick Cowen's themes are of a banality unknown even at Ballad Concerts for which his songs would be too good. Imps and cherubs appear, but the imps wear false noses as obvious as Lord Arthur Pomeroy's, and the cherubs have evidently popped in from the Hippodrome. Yet this scene has the one exquisite line in the play. The girl in her dream wedding-gown advances to her dream-lover and says, " I am ready; you may take me." I can remember no other instance in which Pinero has touched both emotion and simplicity. Probably a gauze curtain and the music of Mr. Norman O'Neill would, between them, have done the trick. And now the couple are fain to expose their new-found beauty, but lo and behold they are ugly as before! Here Sir Arthur, with a laboriousness Sir Marshall Hall would not scorn, cross-examines the only witness to the miracle, who declares that there was never any change except in the spirit. Out of charity they married, and the charity which never faileth has led them to believe all things unto beauty and will lead them to endure all things even unto ugliness. It is to a model with a dramatic sense older than Sir James's that Sir Arthur has turned.

I do not complain, then, of the new armour, but of the old body. The quartet of " mortals " which fills the greater part of the play makes up a lamentable crew. They talk persistently, never-endingly, and all in that curious lingo compounded of the hairdresser and the

leader-writer. Do they talk about darning, then it
becomes " the repair of household linen." The characters " run on " like Flora or Mrs. Nickleby, but alas,
without the wit. Not even ever-charming Miss
Winifred Emery could keep her head above this sorry
stream; she drowned in floods of the unamusing. Mr.
O. B. Clarence, as a tame rector, struggled with a
dreadful figure about an unborn child hovering between
earth and heaven. One by one do the characters, with
midwifely insistence, make unbashful play with this
ornament. Mr. Norman Forbes, in the unfunniest part
ever devised, was funereal; he had obviously given it up.
Miss May Whitty was good as she always is, and equally
good Miss Jean Cadell. I fear me lest, with the range of
parts at present allowed her, the latter actress grow old
before her time. And greatly as I admire her, I should
not cast her for the Angel of the Annunciation. Let me
add that Mr. Nicholas Hannen played a blind Major
with great beauty and feeling. To conclude, little is
wrong with the poetic side of this play which could not
easily be righted. The fairies were a success, " con-
sidering." But no amount of reflection will, I am afraid,
alter the view that Sir Arthur's old mastery of the concrete has declined " by chance or nature's changing
course untrimm'd."

Gentle is as Gentile Doesn't

Loyalties, by John Galsworthy.   St. Martin's Theatre.

MR. GALSWORTHY IS ANOTHER MR. Barlow. You remember how, in the ever-delightful "Sandford and Merton," little Tommy wants to kill the cat which has wickedly devoured his pet robin. Mr. Barlow points out that birds are the lawful prey of cats. Tommy protests that birds are not so cruel. The tutor shows him a sparrow gobbling a worm, and demonstrates that worms are the lawful prey of sparrows. Tommy desires to know what can be done about it, and Mr. Barlow ingeniously arranges for a red-hot gridiron to be placed in front of the next robin's cage for the unnatural edification of the cat. So Mr. Galsworthy. The poor are the natural prey of the rich, the law-breaker of the law-giver, man of his master. What, he wants us to ask ourselves fiercely, are we going to do about it ? And we probably decide that there is no more immediately practicable bar to injustice and oppression than the adoption of the author's outlook of red-hot sympathy. With the resolve, of course, to put that sympathy into practice on the next convenient occasion.

We come away from the typical Galsworthy play feeling that the quarrel has been so magnificently even-handed that nothing could have been done about it. Both sides were equally in the wrong or, as in Greek

134

tragedy, equally in the right. We come away from *Loyalties* with something of the shamefaced feeling of having been discovered looking on at a street fight; a brawl in which we had lacked the courage to intervene on behalf of the weaker combatant. A petty squabble between an unpleasant little Jew who is in the right, and a conventionally pleasant Christian who is hopelessly in the wrong. But right versus wrong is an inversion of the Galsworthian theme proper.

The major Galsworthys always give one the impression of a brain-storm recollected in convalescence. It was touch and go, one suspects, whether the author of *Strife* led his strikers to battle and fell, face to the capitalist, on the flags of Middlesbrough, or whether he sat down to plan what could fairly be said on both sides. Whereas this deft and minor play does not make me feel that the religionist strife which is at its root causes any stir in that passionate bosom. Why cannot man agree to live and let live, whether in the matter of race or country or creed? Call it charity, tolerance, compromise, what you will. Man's inability to achieve a working compromise, his persistence in regarding his own "lights" as the true illumination, and all other perception as the outer darkness, is the keystone of Galsworthian drama, conflicting vision its arch. Its greatest strength has always lain in the author's espousal of each warring cause in turn; his impartial fanaticism. Obviously the virtue peculiar to these plays must be gone out of one in which the author may not take any side at all. It is, we feel, a fluke that Galsworthy was not a Falder nor yet his judge. He might conceivably have been the Jew of *Loyalties*, but not a miracle could

Gentle is as Gentile Doesn't

have made of him the uppish brand of Christian of this play. The Jew, of course, might equally well have been nigger or Chinaman, Chocktaw or Cherokee. Sufficient that he should be fired with the pride of race and, to the distinguished General Canynge, be antipathetic. But to him also the General is an unacquired taste. The author has been extraordinarily fair to De Levis, whom he makes intellectually honest and self-sufficient, less fair to Canynge, who is at once stupid and arrogant. The play begins with the theft of a thousand pounds from De Levis, who is a guest at a country-house party. He has the conviction that the thief is one Captain Ronald Dancy, D.S.O., while the General has proof. What does the General do ? Does he confront Dancy with the evidence ? No. He invites him to make the denial expected of an officer, and pledges his own gentle-manly faith in his innocence, well knowing him to be guilty. *Esprit de corps* such as this seems to me the last refuge of the well-bred scoundrel. " This fellow is one of us, therefore he must not be proved a thief " is not a doctrine to which I can say " Amen." Nor can I think it has the author's blessing. Now De Levis has the very shrewd idea that if the cases had been reversed the General would have gone through his pockets there and then. He proposes to make a fuss. Canynge threatens to turn him out of his clubs—blackmail, which, following on the heels of the similar offence in his last play, shows the author not over-gentle to our aristocracy. Ultimately, out of loyalty to club conven-tions, Dancy is forced to bring his libel action. The General, like Brer Fox, lies low and says nothing about his evidence. Out of loyalty to their respective pro-

Gentle is as Gentile Doesn't

fessions, and the bottom falling out of their case, solicitor and counsel withdraw. Brer Canynge, he try to smuggle Dancy out of the country, giving him a chit to the Spanish War Office containing, presumably, a recommendation for a commission. The police intervene, and Dancy shoots himself.

This, I take it, is thundering bad Galsworthy, but very good anybody else. The play is a good play because, whilst it is going on, and until it is brought to some sort of conclusion, you would rather be in the theatre than anywhere else. In this it resembles those good novels of Miss Braddon which you realized were not masterpieces but which, once taken up, you were reluctant to put down. There is, for instance, a well-calculated and exciting attempt to excuse Dancy. The money was used to satisfy another blackmailer who, being an Italian lodging-house keeper, and not a British General, was inferentially a low fellow. It was also the price obtained by De Levis for a mare which Dancy had given him, and which had no business to run so well afterwards at Kempton. This defence is urged just far enough, and Mr. Eric Maturin's bearing gave it admirable colour. Equally skilful is the drawing of De Levis. He is a fussy, temperamental little cad, a toady yet aggressive, a snob hankering after alien advancement yet aflame with the pride of his own race. No playing of this part could possibly have bettered Mr. Ernest Milton's. He gave you that rare thing in acting, duality, the doubling of the spoken word by an inner emotion. You were moved not so much by what De Levis, under country-house constraint, forced himself to withhold, as by the dumb rancour of centuries. Behind

137

Gentle is as Gentile Doesn't

him was not only the humiliation of the Middle Ages, but the pride it could not shake. The credit here is due more to the actor than the author. When the upstart General threatened to turn De Levis out of the little parish of fashionable London one expected Mr. Milton to round on him with the Roman's " There is a world elsewhere." But then, unlike Coriolanus, the Jew was a snob for whom the universe began at the Ritz and ended at the Savoy. And at the heart of that universe, elevated to the peerage of the clubs, the socially magnificent, intellectually contemptible General Canynge. I have never seen Mr. Dawson Milward so good, so utterly fearless of inferior criticism, so free from self-reproach, so obviously a pillar of the Church, so definitely un-Christian.

Mab and her Friends

Body and Soul, by Arnold Bennett. Regent Theatre.

MR. ARNOLD BENNETT IS THE MOST practically minded man of his generation. Like Mr. Dick, he has ever been prepared to set us right on all manner of subjects; from bathroom taps to How to Live on Twenty-four Hours a Day, from the proper way to read books to the best way to write them. A " fine pragmatic," in Jonson's phrase, his whole lifetime's spirit breathing abhorrence of waste, it is strange that he should at this eleventh hour commit the most wasteful sin of all—the misuse of an opportunity.

The Regent Theatre is the old Euston Music Hall transformed, an immense house situated near the three big railway stations, and in the midst of mean streets. The proprietors, it appears from the programme, are " The Variety Theatres Consolidated, Ltd.," the presenters of the play " The Directors of the Lyric Theatre, Hammersmith." From these nebulous bodies I can disengage only the author, the concrete Mr. Bennett, and the producer, the no less actual Mr. Nigel Playfair. Let me say at once that there is no moral obligation on these gentlemen to behave as altruists and nothing more; that to keep an eye on the main chance is a perfectly proper proceeding. Yet was it necessary, in the circumstances, to stare that chance quite so full in the

face ? One noticed round the doors on that first night
not the usual crowd of comfortably circumstanced idlers,
but a mob many hundreds strong, ragged, ill-condi-
tioned, obviously drawn from the neighbouring slums.
In the midst of all this wretchedness, in its own theatre,
were now installed, not a struggling playwright and
manager striving to keep body and soul together, but
one of the most successful of the world's novelists and
one of the most famous of its producers of plays. I
frankly refuse to believe that the choice of opening piece
was the result of any conscious flouting of responsibili-
ties; I believe simply that their existence had not been
grasped. Yet surely it should have been obvious that a
mass of people whom no playwright had yet addressed,
and a great writer made up a conjunction out of the run
of ordinary commercial enterprise. It is silly to talk of a
" mission " in the theatre. Nobody hates that cant
phrase more than I, yet I am persuaded that if Mr.
Bennett had taken thought he would have explored his
mind for something to worthier purpose than a repetition
of his old gibe at pretty ladies. What's Lady Mab to
the King's Cross railwayman ? He sees her portrait
in the papers, laughs, makes his blunt comment, and
turns to the betting news. He will not, I am convinced,
think it worth his while to visit the Regent Theatre to
watch a display of folly in a cubist drawing-room.

If *Body and Soul* had been presented at a West End
theatre I should stress the point that Lady Mab is not
well done. She is not a fine creature bred out to inanity;
she is not, in fact, bred at all. With a dress which
enwraps the right half of her as though she were an
Eskimo, leaving the left half as bare as a South Sea

Mab and her Friends

Islander, she is the Lady Mab of the little dressmaker's imaginings. Fielding, revelling over Lady Booby, left us in no doubt that she was a person of quality. Mr. Bennett's play is the literary counterpart of that gesture whereby the street-urchin shows his contempt for the quality. What good is this talk about Psychology to the corner-boys of the Euston Road? In the lexicon of those bright youths there's no such word; at best they will confuse it with the horse of that name which let them down so badly in this year's Derby. I cannot think that even that poor thing, the main chance, has been well served. The first-night audience was of a "brilliance" purely migratory; you would have said the St. James's. It applauded jokes which, at that theatre, would have been welcome. I doubt, however, whether the little Camden Town typist, whose endeavours to refine her speech result in such enormities as "tape-rater," is likely to be amused by her prototype on the stage. By some extraordinary accident the pilgrimage to Hammersmith "caught on." (Let us not be gammoned by a plea as to the merit of *The Beggar's Opera*. There's a queer element of luck in these matters. *Diff'rent*, a magnificent play, magnificently acted, brought no crowds to Hampstead.) Either Mr. Playfair is relying upon a repetition of the miracle, or he must believe Mr. Bennett's fantasy to be suited to the former patrons of the Euston Music Hall. But plays which are to draw the Euston Road must, I submit, offer comment upon life as that road knows it, convey emotion which it can understand. There is one admirable character in the play, the Mayoress of Bursley, most beautifully played by Miss Dora Gregory. This is the humanity

to which Mr. Bennett brings tenderness, humour, and
his sterling Midland grit; it is the one side of life
which reveals him as the great artist. Nothing could
be truer than the Mayoress's self-possessed " I've a
duty to per-form, Ezra, and I shall per-form it. I shall
keep my place, and I shall see as her ladyship keeps
hers." This is true, even in the Euston Road. As
soon as this writer touches smarter London, fineness
and sensitiveness depart; his satirical writing hangs
on him like the Sunday clothes of his Midland gawks.
I sometimes think that Mr. Bennett despises the theatre;
it is certainly the vehicle which he chooses for his least
emotional work. And the theatre, whenever it detects
this, will take its revenge and decline to take Mr. Bennett to its bosom. Emotion is that which a theatre-
audience will have. Bad or false emotion is, in this
medium, better than none. The melodramatic excesses
of the Brothers Melville, Mr. Chevalier's *My Old
Dutch*, Miss Dell's *The Way of an Eagle* are better plays
than *Body and Soul*. I will even say that they are more
artistic, since they stick more closely to that old dictum
of Aristotle, that the artist shall consent to his medium.
The audience at a popular theatre is part of the medium.

At the Regent Theatre we are invited to laugh at
Lady Mab. The " brilliant " first-nighters made the
allowances necessitated by her bringing up, but I am
afraid future audiences will take her for inconsiderable
trash and no more. Her talk of earning her own living
is playwright's bunkum. She does not know how to
make a cup of tea or scrub a floor, her only practicable
walk in life is the shameful perambulation. If the play
were the least little bit convincing, if it were not

swaddled in spoof, spiritualism, and quackery, I should
declare it to be the very torch of mob-incendiarism.   If
the working classes had only a few brains they would,
after the performance, repair to Park Lane and pull the
houses about their plutocratic owners' ears and noses.
If they had more brains they would do this by Act of
Parliament.   If they had still more they would not pull
down palaces, but build up cottages.   But inasmuch as
they have no brains at all, they will just guffaw.   Or
rather, a few of them will make that delectable noise;
the others will continue to find the betting news more
interesting.   I hope only that they will guffaw with, and
not at, Miss Viola Tree, whose performance brought a
lump into my throat.   It was, oh! so utterly well-
intentioned and hopeless, conscientious and helpless.
Miss Tree is a dear, and it was naughty of Mr. Bennett
to use her so.   The part of the typist might with advantage be cut up in little bits and sent round the music-
halls.   Miss Nan Marriott Watson was very good as the
'cute little shopgirl, but does Mr. Bennett imagine that
Bursley would, in the wildest clodhoppings of its
imagination, have mistaken the typist for the daughter
of a marquess ?   Actors have hitherto considered Gold-
smith's overshadowed Hastings as the worst part ever
inflicted on a mime.   Mr. Bennett's Aaron Draper is
streets ahead of him in futility, and my heart went out
to Mr. Martin Walker as he struggled with his long
cadenza of inanition.

A New Percy Ballad

If Four Walls Told, by Edward Percy. Savoy Theatre.

AMONG THE MORE AMIABLE PRE-dilections of pedantry is the passion—drat the p's—for using words in their primary signification. Take that ordinary word "critic." My dictionary gives a twofold definition: 1, a person *able to discuss*; one skilled in judging of literary or artistic merit; 2, one who censures or finds fault; a harsh examiner; a caviller. The pedant rejoices in 1, common acceptation has fastened upon 2. The use of the word in its debased or carping sense reduces your adventurer in search of masterpieces to a prosecutor of niggling imperfections. This degradation does not lack authority, some of the most famous writers showing deplorable laxity in respect of this word. "Paint to cathedral scale!" Balzac makes one artist say to another. "Paint something big and silence the critics!" Now Balzac knew better than any other that the best in this line, say his own Claude Vignon, give freest tongue in the presence of the masterpiece. If, in art, there be an incontrovertible truth, it is that the critic is known by his power of appreciation; not only by his ecstasy in presence of the first-rate, but by his power to pick out the gold in something which is not even second-rate. The best criticism is a hunt for buried treasure; every good dramatic critic signs Jim Hawkins. His visits to

the theatre are voyages of discovery; out puts he for a
new play as it were a Treasure Island, knowing the
ascending curtain shall reveal the cache. Though he
have Sarcey's years, yet has he a boy's heart. That
jaded air, or familiar look of dissembling pickpocket, is a
disguise to hoodwink the vestibule, the mask beneath
which the pirate conceals his find. But joy is ill to
hide. I know in an instant whether my colleagues'
hang-dog air is mere luckless assumption or the real
misery of drawing blank. In the theatre the pedant
must have his way; the critic is that happy fellow, the
discoverer and judge of merit.

At the first night of *If Four Walls Told* there was, they
tell me, no effort at critical deception. None could be
jealous of another. The precious metal was scattered
about the stage to be lifted at ease by the least experienced of buccaneers. I saw this village comedy for the
first time on the occasion of its hundredth performance,
and liked it enormously. For conscience' sake I must
declare it to be not the entire, perfect, and rather tedious
chrysolite, but that more exciting thing, a gem carelessly
cut yet exquisitely set. For that which matters least
in the play is its central idea. The author sets out with a
problem which would have been dear to the heart of
Ibsen himself. Liz Rysing has lost her only child.
Jan, her husband, proposes that they should adopt a
daughter, and is strangely insistent that it shall be the
seventeen-year-old love-child of a woman in the village.
Liz is unwilling to believe that Jan is Hope Tregon-
ning's father. Ultimately she taxes him with the faith-
lessness which is concealment and, eager to believe his
half-admission, hits him in the face. This scene is very

well prepared. "I've laid awake night after night thinking of the lads out on the waters. Them two lives I made . . ." thus preludes an old wife. That Jan would adopt a life of his making, not of hers, rankles in the bosom of Liz, who can bear no more children. Hunger and jealousy is the theme then, which, no sooner stated, peters out. The second act is concerned with a shipwreck and the supposed loss of Jan. What follows is a more or less harrowing replica of *Riders to the Sea*. Liz, we think, must lose her reason—a conjecture to which Miss Edyth Goodall's intensity gives support—whilst for the third act there remains a restatement of *La Joie fait Peur*, or the Overjoy of the Return. To the general surprise, Jan turns up wet but undrowned, with another act to go. What, now, is to become of our problem? Ibsen, we realize, would have begun his play with the action over and done with, and only the mental conflict to come. What a nose had the old boy for scenting the heart of a mystery! He would have rung up his curtain on a peasant Rita Allmers wringing sodden duds and her hands at the discovery that the sea in giving up her husband had not solved her problem. And for three mortal hours she and we would have had to face that problem. *Little Hope* our Henrik would probably have called the play. But Mr. Edward Percy has left himself only forty minutes in which to tidy up some inessential matters concerning the identity of the man who was actually drowned, and the real fathership of the child. We gather that he will burke his major problem, and, in effect, he does.

What happened, I imagine, is that, in mid-travail, Mr. Percy fell in love with the other characters and

A New Percy Ballad

basely threw over Liz. He has an enchanting study of a fireside egoist, senile, slippered, garrulous. To Mr. Reginald Bach, the creator of the rôle, the author dedicates his play, after the manner of Rostand and Coquelin. But whereas Cyrano was avowedly the soul of the play, David is not. Or has become so by an afterthought. Mr. Percy, enamoured of a precious ornament, worked away at it until, in the end, it dwarfed the construction which it was designed to embellish. Balzac has a story about a painter who overloads his canvas until nothing remains. Mr. Percy is luckier than Frenhofer; he has stippled away his original conception, but replaced it with a thousand little dots and touches of delight. His minor characters are faithfully observed and abound in naturalness and the good tang of peasant humour. Implication lurks in unexpected turns of speech. " What you've got against my mother isn't that she did wrong but that she suffered wrong," says little Hope to a monster of pretending rectitude. The old sorner bridles, and flounces out of the room with an indignant " This ain't no place for a God-fearing, Christian woman!" Thus delivers herself Puritanical Discretion. A natural Good-Deeds, who finds delight in eating, drinking, singing, loving, looks after her and says contemptuously " The Christian pig!" So, rudely yet decently, is the true religion restored. The old woman was admirably enacted by Miss Ethel Coleridge, the riot in her gait fenced in by a hypocritical skirt, prudery in her mask contending with natural sluttishness. Mr. Ambrose Manning looked, and acted, like a Toby-jug of the best period. I did not see Mr. Bach's David; Mr. Laurence Hannay's was excellent. I do

A New Percy Ballad

not blame Mr. Percy for taking these people to his heart; if they obtrude upon the play's chief interest they are nevertheless delightful interlopers.

I come with some diffidence to Miss Goodall's Liz, and this for the reason that the part deals hardly by this excellent actress. Liz must work up to great heights of emotion, with the knowledge that half-way through the play she is to be left suspended in mid-air. Lacking a permanent power of levitation it is perhaps too much to expect that an actress will not soar whilst yet she may. Some of the tones which Miss Goodall uses to accompany her flight are of the sepulchral order we associate with Mrs. Siddons. And just as that overwhelming personage demanded of the chimney-pots " How gat they there ? " so are we inclined to ask how, in this sentimental comedy, gat the poor girl to those heights of anguish. Or rather, how gat she down again ? Only the interval knows. Again, Liz is condemned to sit at a table grief-stricken, motionless, and mum, whilst the company indulge in comic humours. In *Justice* Miss Goodall showed that she can gather agony in her eyes, but then the talk was relevant. Here it is irrelevant. Our great Siddons would not have stood this. "Silence, dolts!" she would have thundered. Miss Goodall never thunders, but she tolls her sentences like a passing bell. She reiterated the descending phrase about the " clean . . . white . . . sheet" with such awful insistence that my brain took un-lawful refuge in another dying fall of three . . . blind . . . mice. But it was not the actress's fault. When-ever Mr. Percy allowed Liz a spell of relief from agoniz-ing, no playing could have bettered Miss Goodall's.

Some Film-Emotions and a Moral

HE FOUR HORSEMEN OF THE *Apocalypse*, taken in conjunction with some recent multipopulous films, suggests that this vast industry has at last found its artistic feet. Just as, after a time, the motor-car designer got away from the idea of the horse, and discovered the shape of a mechanically propelled vehicle to be implicit in its motive power, so the latest film-producers are finding that pantomime and a flat projection have given them a medium independent of, and insubservient to, the theatre. It was recognized from the first, if not by the producer at least by the onlooker, that if the screen was to be an art at all it must do other than hold the camera up to a stageful of dumb actors; the difficulty was to discover the essential difference. The "cowboy" films had not got beyond pointing the lens at the circus, while those grandiose displays of passion, degenerate dramas of the fatty heart, pantagraphic enlargements of the comedies of Tom Robertson, were obviously not more than the old obsession of the theatre at its most burdensome. And with the enormous growth of popularity and the use of the largest halls came the feeling, again on the part of the onlooker, that the medium was capable of wider scope than the elaboration of the millionaire-magnate's passion for the typist whose fiancée was falsely accused of robbing the safe. Of this feeling the producer became, at length, dimly aware.

When Reinhardt, in *The Miracle*, sent his company of nuns up-stage as though he were flushing a covey of white-winged birds, he did more than increase the effectiveness obtained by a single figure; he translated emotion from the particular into the general. When I first read of these " super films," how *Intolerance* had cost a million dollars—or was it pounds ?—how the " set " for the chariot races in *The Queen of Sheba* covered one hundred and fifty acres, how a single scene of *Theodora* contained fourteen thousand actors— frankly, I was inclined to scoff. This, I thought, could be but producer's vulgarity, the old desire to stagger the universe and catch its pence. Then when I saw the films I realized that, behind the ostentation, lay more than a display of numbers. It was Reinhardt's idea all over again, the conferring of unity upon a crowd, the transformation of a rabble into an entity. Of course, so big a thing as this was not to be achieved at once, nor without mistakes. The story of *Theodora* was uncommonly like the novelette of a kitchen maid who should be afflicted with sentimental elephantiasis; the fourteen thousand characters were too small individually, and so not more impressive that the little people who stroll about at the foot of an architect's elevation. The theme of *The Queen of Sheba* was that of an overgrown feuilleton with a philandering Solomon for hero. Here again the crowd, at rest, was not more significant than a photograph of Mr. Henry Ford's work people during the dinner hour. In action as when, for instance, it

Some Film-Emotions and a Moral

leaped the arena walls and swarmed at the heels of the
scudding chariots, it took on a quality which no crowd
in the theatre can give, yet which remained decorative,
and not more than decorative. But in that other film,
Intolerance, the armies of Cyrus and Belshazzar had
swept the screen not only with the purely embellishing
quality of the passage-work in the overtures to "Oberon"
and "Euryanthe," but also with something of the fate-
ful implications of the Fifth Symphony.

So far I cannot claim that the innovation was really
more than spectacular. No stage-manager, however
clever, can convey a mass emotion to which the audience
cannot, in the nature of things, be susceptible. Belshazzar and Cyrus lived too long ago for us to take sides.
Whereas the emotion of *The Four Horsemen* is very
recent, almost too recent for artistic purposes. (One of
the sub-titles suggested very tactfully that *there*, in that
other country, soldiers were arming in the full conviction
and consciousness of right. The fact remains that I
should not invite a guest from that country to witness
this film. It sears the mind with old memories that
were better forgotten, and reopens old wounds that
were better healed. Probably this is unavoidable. You
cannot stir up national emotion and take only the gilt-
edged, sentimental prettiness.) I do not want to write
too loosely or impracticably of this " mass emotion."
Obviously, it cannot meander about unshackled, magnoperating in the void. It must be harnessed to some
kind of story. This, in *The Four Horsemen*, is just a
trifle mechanical. The invention of an old rancher of
the Argentine, whose two daughters marry, one a
Frenchman and the other a German, is an unnecessarily

elaborate device for getting the two races into the most intimate of all conflicts. It was managed much more simply in *Les Oberle* and the *Burgomaster of Stilemonde*; but it may be that the producers were not aiming at economy. And perhaps there was no reason why they should so aim; there is virtue in extravagance as well as in cheese-paring. The story, as it is told up to the outbreak of the war, is good, unsubtle, yet not vulgar. As soon, however, as the drum-taps speak, we know that we are to listen to a more poignant language.

One felt curiously divided on this matter of a personal core to a world upheaval. At times it seemed absurdly trivial; at other times one reflected that people do not, actually, visualize events in the mass, but only through the medium of their personal outlook. I have already said that the story is not vulgar; I want to say now that it is of common application. This tale of a Francesca enamoured of a Paolo and married to a Malatesta whom she does not love, this story of a conflict between eager passion and duty to a stricken husband is as old as the hills, and has never known solution. But war, too, is old and has that same element of conflicting right. You take away all dignity from those years if you deny the German breast the same flame as that which animated the French. I do not know of any film in which the actual and the symbolical have been better interwoven. To bring those four figures—Conquest, War, Famine, and Death—upon the screen and keep silliness at arm's length was, in itself, a triumph, whilst the implications of the last few moments required and obtained very delicate handling. Sometimes in a big picture the smallest things are the most effective; a

Some Film-Emotions and a Moral

French flag borne by a peasant in pitiful defence of his village caught me by the throat.

Yet this film, like so many others, has the annoying trick of leading the spectator right up to the brink of intellectual interest and then fobbing him off. It gives him a glimpse of those sinister personages typical of the brain of the hostile command, and immediately switches him off to the consideration of a boor in his bath. There is an exquisite moment when the weary troops come to the fountain to drink. The mind wants to linger here, to bait, as it were, with these jaded beasts of the inhuman burden. But alas! elsewhere there is fooling toward, which we are not allowed to miss. The screen is still shy of absolute beauty. And this for two reasons. Either the producers of pictures are afraid of their audiences, or they do not know beauty when they see it. Both suppositions are, I think, true. A friend of mine, a considerable artist, who was asked to write a scenario for an all-British film of film-producers, was offered a free hand in every respect but one. There was to be no subtlety. " Any muck you like so long as the situations are strong. Plenty of heart interest, but no sex stuff. Above all, no subtlety. They won't stand for it! "

" Sit for it, you mean," answered my friend.

Then, raising his voice, " And you can keep your all-British commission, Mr. Hiram K. Meschügge! "

These American gentlemen at present in control of the recreative provender of the great mass of the people, wielding a power for aesthetic good or evil equal, probably, to that of all the printing presses in the world, are amazingly ignorant.

" Say," said one of these unlettered magnates after he

had been watching Lucien Guitry throughout four acts of *Pasteur*, " say, who's that guy ? "

One would despair for the future of any art so largely in the hands of these tasteless American producers if it were not that, up to the present, they undoubtedly lead. (I write this without knowledge of the Norwegian and Swedish films which, I am told, are extraordinarily good.) Sometimes behind the horn spectacles of our cousins I think I detect faint glimmerings that the world may hold scope for other activities besides stooping to pick up the almighty dollar. It is as though our cousins were harking back to some word or thing remembered from a former existence, yet of which the meaning has long been lost. " Beauty ! " they cry, " that's what the darned thing was called." And they proceed to give " beauty " publicity, whether their work possesses it or not. Of *The Four Horsemen of the Apocalypse* they announce : "Shakespeare in Music ; Wagner in Pictures ; Michael Angelo in Words." *C'est gigantesque !* as Flaubert used to observe of some bourgeois enormity.

There is an admirable moment in *Theodora* in which the Empress, stabbing Marcellus, drives the dagger home with her shoulder blades, and thus forces the weight of her body to do blindly that which she was afraid to watch her hand accomplish. At once the screen flashes :

> " And on the morrow
> Came Theodora to the villa
> After a sleepless night."

This, the lingo of the patent-medicine advertisement, is, I suppose, " Michael Angelo in words."

Some Film-Emotions and a Moral

In *Nero*, at the Philharmonic Hall, I found no trace of emotion except that which one had thought safely buried with Wilson Barrett. The film is our old friend, *The Sign of the Cross*, all over again. History repeating itself, a matinée is to be given for the benefit of the clergy, but not, presumably, to the ultimate loss of the management. Doubtless it is hoped that some bishop will get him on his hind legs and bray about this film, some rural dean give forth ruridecanal encomiums. Alas, for the purposes of boosting, that Mr. Gladstone is not alive! Under the cloak of religion *Nero* makes considerable display of sensuality. How, it may be objected, can a writer give virtue its sad meed unless he shows vice in its brightest colours ? (Sir Hall Caine used constantly to find himself in this convenient difficulty.) And therefore while the Christian maidens are of a flickering innocence bordering on the imbecile the pagan *roués* must perambulate Rome with the frenzy of stags in the rutting season, their eyeballs bursting from their sockets. The story, says the programme, " agrees with the account of Nero's life as related by," among others, Suetonius! This is like saying that *Little Arthur's* ingenuous account of our own Edward the Second tallies with Marlowe. Nero is a case for the expert in psychosis, not for the scenario-monger. He is essentially an improper hero for the screen.

If we must present Nero in the theatre—to which before an educated audience there can be no objection— then let us have the Sadist, the man whom the Nonconformist conscience would undoubtedly call mad, and the Antichrist of Christian tradition. But let us also have the pupil of Seneca, the emperor, and the artist. How good or bad an artist Nero was can never be established. Personally I am inclined to think he would have been very much at home in Chelsea. *Qualis artifex pereo* shows that he was at least preoccupied with matters other than sensuality and butchery. And in coming to any necessarily preposterous and essentially pernickety judgment of a Great Man, whose greatness in the Wildean sense—Jonathan, not Oscar—lingered in the popular imagination for ten centuries after his death, let us, for the sake of common sense, remember the time.

I think it is Des Esseintes in Huysmans's novel who complains that the projects which a Nero would have carried out must, in our more squeamish day, come to iniquitous fulfilment in the brain alone. Given the absolute power of a Nero, Mr. Pussyfoot Johnson would, I doubt not, prove himself the greater tyrant. Of all the great men of the past Nero is he whom I should most like to meet. Away with your pale Emersons, Lincolns, and the whole anaemic caboodle. Better for a race to be destroyed by an emperor with blood in him than to have prohibition thrust upon it by some sanctimonious economist with ginger-beer in his veins.

The Nero of the present film is a compromise false equally to virtue as to vice. The French actor, Gretillat, gives the torso and the jowl cleverly enough; de Max would have added the hermaphroditic complex, the brains, and the descent from Augustus. But the whole atmosphere of the picture suggests, not the decadence which was the Eternal City, but the tawdriness which is the modern Palais de Danse—a Rome too obviously built in a day.

Why, I wonder, must all screen heroines be feeble-

Some Film-Emotions and a Moral

minded ? The heroine of *The Game of Life*, at the West End Cinema, is blind from birth, and believes that everybody else is blind too. Her world is one in which a man must touch a thing before he can know it, and if he would speak of an elephant, must first produce one. A student of Braille, she does not know the word " sight," and is confounded when some careless fellow says that he can see the stars. " What is ' see ' ? " she lisps.

Smilin' Through, at the Marble Arch Pavilion, is feeble, pretentious, and lachrymose. A bride who has been shot by a jealous lover during the wedding ceremony—which the producer places in the back-garden—spends the next fifty years or so " on the other side," hovering about in an expectant bridal gown. When her spirit is not hovering it is reincarnated in a flesh-and-blood niece, her sister's child. The sister also " goes over " later on, and the two indulge in sentimental colloquy. Watching this rubbish I thought regretfully of that play of Mr. Laurence Housman in which a departed Victorian lady wires from earth to an elder sister who has preceded her—the address is that of a distinctly anthropomorphic Heaven—" Railway accident. Arriving 4.30." " I expected you earlier," says the elder lady, looking at the clock and pecking her sister's cheek. " The train was late," replies the younger woman simply. Oh, for just one little breath of Mr. Housman's irony, or even of his common sense, to blow away these screen absurdities! " Does irony go out with life ? " asks Lamb. Alas! that it goes out or ever we enter the grave, as soon, indeed, as we set foot in the cinema! Miss Norma Talmadge dies from a

157

Some Film-Emotions and a Moral

gunshot wound with less show of emotion than one of
Messrs. Lyons's waitresses exhibits on receiving an
order for a cup of tea. According to the programme
this actress "reveals a spiritual power that goes far
beyond acting." This is nonsense. Miss Talmadge
smiles prettily and weeps prettily; that is all. And in
this film she bears the peculiarly detestable name of
" Moonyeen! " The sub-titles and accompanying
music are a very nightmare of banality. Tosti in
pictures, Miss Dell in music, and in words that New
Oxford Street sculptor whose effigies proclaim Somebody's Sustentative Belts—that, I must think, is more
nearly the truth about such films as this.

It was pleasant, by way of contrast, to sit in quiet
enjoyment at the Stoll Picture Theatre, Kingsway, of
some unpretentious domestic pieces, including *General
John Regan*, with Mr. Milton Rosmer. There was also
a magnificent picture of rival pirate gangs cutting each
other's throats in a sunken submarine. This was a fine
example of the proper function of the screen which,
when it is not magnoperating in mass emotion, is to
supplement, not supplant, the theatre, and to show
aspects of life and drama that defy Drury Lane. " Blow,
winds, and crack your cheeks! " should be inscribed
over all shadowy portals. Cataracts and hurricanoes
are the thing here, with incident piled on incident. Let
the film-actor leave that little matter of psychology to
the Duses who, I dare swear, would make a poor show
of their minds' insides at fathom five, or thereabout.

" Stroheim is no more to be shunned as a contribution
to art than Hogarth's ' Rake's Progress,' Balzac's
' Comédie Humaine,' Dante's ' Inferno,' or Ibsen's

' Ghosts.' " Again the giant enormity. The moral of *Foolish Wives*, which is " Written, Directed by, and Featuring Stroheim "—*what* a lot these " literary " producers are!—is that wealthy American ladies should not, whilst at Monte Carlo, pay midnight visits to Russian Counts living at the top of high towers unprovided with fire escapes, whose jealous maidservants are waiting to destroy them with petrol. There is no objection to the screen being didactic; it had better be that than pseudo-psychological. Remarking one day to a companion upon the close attention which a film-audience gave to a performance of the middle and last movements of the Mendelssohn Violin Concerto, I observed that the piece was probably new to them. " Not only the piece," answered my friend, " it's the first time they've heard the fiddle! " There was a grain of truth in this. Dotted about the house there may be a Cabinet Minister or two, but collectively the cinema audience is totally uneducated. They gape before the screen as the thirteenth-century playgoer gaped before the morality-play. And *Foolish Wives* is a poor morality. A woman who visits a chance acquaintance at midnight with ninety thousand francs loose in her pocket is, if she be innocent-minded, too big a fool to be worth our while. Or say she is worth the police-court missionary's while, and not Balzac's, Ibsen's, or Dante's. Such a woman becomes interesting as soon as she is shown to be not innocent but aware, teased by her passions and their willing dupe. A woman of thirty-five who allows herself to be decoyed, even at Monte Carlo, and pays for her rape into the bargain, is an intolerable fool who deserves no better fate. Let her put down her ninety thousand francs in the knowledge that Russian Counts are an expensive luxury, and we should at once leave yawning and begin to attend. Such a film wouldn't be "moral." I am not concerned with that; it is conceivable that it might be true. Whereas the present film is neither true nor moral. It is untrue to suggest that any normal woman can be such a fool as this victim of Stroheim. It is untrue to life to suggest that rape, sentimental and physical, and nothing but rape, fills the mind of the average woman to the exclusion of everything else. *Foolish Wives* is, in this respect, almost uncannily immoral.

I wish people would get it out of their heads that a film is made respectable by the fact that the villain comes to a disastrous end. Stroheim's fate is no worse than that of hundreds of thousands during the past ten years. He was a professional seducer whose seductions were extraordinarily successful. By seduction the fellow fulfilled his being and was happy. To make the film moral he should have been unhappy. Stroheim's end was purely accidental; whereas the fate of many a decent, honourable, blameless fellow during the war was quite perfectly inevitable. A moral film, I repeat, would have shown Stroheim made unhappy by his vice.

Here again we are up against a piece of cant too generally accepted. The reader may remember an old picture, "The Child: and What He will Become." On the left of the picture is the head of a boy, before whom lies the choice between good and evil. To the right are parallel lines of heads of which the upper series represents School, College, Industry, Success, and Honourable Old Age; the lower Playing Truant, the

Some Film-Emotions and a Moral

Streets, Vice, Misery and Wretchedness, Beggary and Despair. Thus the Idle and the Industrious Apprentice. The terms of reference in both are purely financial. If the little fellow in the modern daub had been born with ten thousand a year and a strong constitution, I imagine he could have run the whole gamut of vice to a dishonourable and happy old age. Why cannot we look the truth in the face and realize that virtue and only virtue makes virtuous people happy, and equally that vice and only vice makes vicious people happy. Contrariwise, that while vice makes the virtuous unhappy, virtue makes the vicious uncomfortable. You cannot, of course, make any sort of film out of virtue. Virtuous people, like happy countries, have no history. How, it is important to ask, can we make a *moral* and yet true film out of vice ? By making the vicious unhappy ? That would not be true, as we have seen; the best we can do is to make them poor. But Stroheim wasn't poor. By his single eyeglass he made more money in five minutes than a dozen men can accumulate in a dozen lifetimes lived after the precepts of Samuel Smiles. The producer or scenario-monger who would make a film about Stroheim must choose between that which is untrue and moral, and that which is true and immoral. *Foolish Wives*, as usual in the cinema, makes the worst of both worlds, and is both untrue and immoral. The simple, sobering verity is that in this world vice is its own reward, and often a very good one. I defy any film-producer to put that on the screen and make it look proper.

This film is really a highly amusing masque, the incidents are exciting, the photography is first-class.

Some Film Emotions and a Moral

Stroheim himself is a fine actor, the personification of Junkerdom, the Prussian *pur sang*, and no Slav. " A man you will love to hate," runs the announcement, with an eye to the little scullery maid. For myself I should hate not to love Stroheim; he is so well acted. The film has been cut stupidly. This Don Juan worthy of Hogarth, Balzac, Dante, Ibsen—and why not Byron, Baudelaire, and Mr. Gilbert Frankau ?—is bundled into a sewer in less time than a competent actor can say " A rat ! " Whereas the impersonation has been powerful enough for me to want a sub-title which shall proclaim :

" And now I'll do't: and so he goes to . . . hell !"

A Little Pot of Jelly

Husbands are a Problem, by Harris Deans.
Ambassadors Theatre.
The Limpet, by Vernon Woodhouse and Victor
MacClure. Kingsway Theatre.

" LITTLE POT OF JELLY BEST FITS a little belly," the conceit of a seventeenth-century poet making offering to his mistress, comes into my mind whenever I see a little comedy in a little room. There is a subtle relationship between play and theatre to which we do not always pay sufficient attention. Greek drama owes much of its essential nobility not to an exalted kink in the Greek mind, but to the fact that it was declaimed to a multitude seated in hollows scooped out of the rock of a hill-side. Now intimacies at a distance become trivialities, and to bawl trivialities in the Dionysiac theatre at Athens to thirty thousand grave Greeks half-listening to the play, half-contemplating Hymettus and the blue Ægean Sea, would be worse than dinning commonplaces about the weather into the ear of a deaf old lady. The poet had to find something on a big scale and of general interest. It might be suggested that intimacy's opportunity came with the advent of the strolling player. He, you remember, improvised his stage in the courtyard of an inn, the galleries of which were reserved for the quality, whilst the vulgar huddled together in the pit. Off-hand, you might say that here was the chance for delicate hints and subtleties, confidences *à demi-mot*. A trifle of reflection, and you realize that anything which the actor might wish to convey from the cover of his right hand to the spectator in the gallery seated, not metaphorically but actually, directly above his right ear, must by that very gesture be withheld from the person in the pit standing immediately below his left foot. From this of necessity proceeded a breadth of style which had a complete meaning from above and below and also on three sides at once; hence, too, the robustious school of drama. Intimacy, one must think, is probably a quite modern invention in the theatre.

Two little plays of the entirely confidential order, *Husbands are a Problem*, at the Ambassadors Theatre, and *The Limpet*, at the Kingsway, pleased me enormously but after a different manner. It occurs to me that the difference in these two ways of liking may explain why the first play had to be withdrawn, whilst the second runs merrily. To begin with, the Ambassadors is the cosiest theatre in London. The entrance to the stalls is almost flush with the curtain, and you at once perceive the well of the orchestra to be so narrow that if two would play the fiddle one must sit behind. I attended an afternoon performance and, as soon as the curtain rose, was glad of my tweeds. Obviously this was not a formal play, but a jolly country-house party. You sat, a little silent perhaps, tired after your two rounds of golf, in a corner of Mrs. Ripley's pleasant drawing-room and listened to the chatter of the tea-table, feeling that if you interrupted your hostess's inconsequential flow with a " Nonsense, dear lady! " she would turn

A Little Pot of Jelly

delightedly to meet the unexpected attack and repulse it with original wit. Miss Kate Cutler has the secret of artificiality—consistency. She is careful never to obtrude the smallest hint of real emotion. Towards the end the author is obliged by the pattern of his play to beg of his chief interpreter at least a simulation of sentiment. Miss Cutler makes the concession gracefully, but we realize that, whisper the o'erfraught heart as dutifully as she may, it is never in the least danger of breaking. Mrs. Ripley's absurdities are entirely logical; inapt to the many varying situations, they are consistent with a single unvarying mentality. Reasoning, so to speak, on her head, the quasi-foolish lady is "all of a piece." Telegrams, she complains, are sexless things, meaning that people do not put "Mr." or "Mrs." on the envelope. Succinctly she sums up the attitude of the churches towards divorce in a disjointed "Catholics are so peculiar." She repels her daughter's suggestion of another woman, and vaguely murmurs incompatibility, desertion, cruelty. "Was there cruelty?" asks the daughter. "My dear, they *proved* it," replies Mrs. Ripley with the most triumphant conviction. And she knows perfectly well, and you know too, that finger was never lifted against her. Bethinking herself as she outlines some peculiarly outrageous project, she cries, "I knew I had forgotten something! My reputation!" and thereby establishes a "niceness" which would satisfy even the very proper old ladies of Mr. Wells's Bladesover. There is social criticism here. It seemed to me that in Mrs. Ripley Mr. Harris Deans had not only brought off a very fine piece of observation, but had kept it very skilfully in the key of comedy. I

A Little Pot of Jelly

did not lament the lack of action. Strong though the spider's web of comedy may be, the gossamer of intellectual folly can never successfully resist the strain of bodily fooling which is farce. Miss Cutler at her most rapier-like, Mr. C. V. France countering with the bludgeon of pure good nature—between them these two fine artists put up a delicate battle of the comic spirit. The wielder of the clumsier weapon is the most likeable of actors. "We shall obey, were she ten times our mother," was always a good maxim. I should be always obedient to the charm of Mr. France were he, which is not possible, a ten times better actor.

The play at the Kingsway is also amusing, but less intimately so. The shape of the house does not pour attention upon the stage quite in the same way as, at the Ambassadors, do those cup-like stalls and tilting circle. The theatre is larger, and to " get over " calls for a different kind of playing. Mr. Stanley Turnbull is, physically, a very large actor indeed, and imposes his genial personality on the audience with equal insistence to that with which, in the play, he forces his odious presence on his hosts. Monumentally loathsome to the other characters, to us Joe Sheepwell is a mountain of delight. His tongue drops fatness, as Hazlitt said of another man of bulk who was also a sorner, but it is a fatness which has turned rancid in the mouth. In the chambers of this sponger's brain it " snows of meat and drink " of other people. It is good to see so broad a cartoon on the finical West End stage, and playgoers should be grateful to Messrs. Vernon Woodhouse and Victor MacClure. The type which they have portrayed belongs not to an age but to all time. Unsnubbable in London to-day as in the Rome of two thousand years ago, Sheepwell would not have been lost upon the crowd in the theatre of Plautus, nor, in the Elizabethan courtyard, would he have failed to " make good." There is that unction in his enactor's voice which not even the primitive mask could obscure, whilst, contrariwise, his countenance is sufficiently expressive to stand transference to the screen. This actor's bow of vulgarity has two strings; heard but not glimpsed, seen but unheard, he would convey to the simplest mind an impression of appalling, and delightful, commonness. Whereas Miss Cutler's more subtle art, depending for its effectiveness on a marriage of magpie gesture and raven intonation, must be both seen and heard. Like Réjane, this very clever actress with admirable calculation croaks herself hoarse upon the battlements of realistic comedy. Like the Frenchwoman she uses her adorably false intonations to suggest the morass of an uncultivated mind. This is something which the screen can never give; for so fine an art as this appreciation must be sophisticated.

Any Child's Play

A Children's Pantomime. New Oxford Theatre.

HOW MUCH, I WONDER, OF MR. Cochran's " First Children's Pantomime," at the New Oxford Theatre, is really suited to the child-mind ? *Tot homunculi, quot sententiae.* Of two like manikins let me concede that one will be ravished by Poiret, the French dressmaker, and Stowitts, the Russian choreographist. But give me leave to think that the other may put a polite little hand before its rosy mouth. When Turgenev, who would have written a " book " after Mr. Cochran's own heart, made up fairy-stories for little nephews and nieces, serpents and toads, it is related, issued from his lips and fell writhing and spitting upon the ground. The English child, however, is of a more stolid temperament, and prefers the plain song of a plain nurse to the fine embroideries of the artist. The story of his pantomime should be told as simply as possible. Its setting should be a glorification of commonplace things. Children adore those old-fashioned ballets transfigurative of the familiar, those arrangements of nursery mugs and platters, of personages and plates in well-known storybooks, of flowers encountered in walks abroad. To them a mechanical change from winter to summer is worth a wilderness of Baksts and Gauguins.

Any Child's Play

In the interest of the children you may caricature and anthropomorphize animals with impunity. The more extravagant the travesty, the more heartsome the laughter. Let him who plays the hind legs of the cow dance a human hornpipe; let his prior emulate Tishy at the starting-gate and cross a scornful leg. But let not your cubist fellow draw a house which could not possibly stand up. Those who have played with bricks upon a floor know better. I hasten to say that Messrs. Henri and Laverdet are no Dada-ists. Their scenes have beauty, but it is of a kind disquietingly post-Victorian. It is later than the children. The actors, of course, must be such as tickled parents when they were taken to the pantomime. The " principal boy " shall be a harridan infamously opulent, over-caparisoned, and over-plumed. " Down the pink champaign of her chops "—to quote a Georgian poet—the ostrich feather, monstrous, droops. The " principal girl " shall be a dream of inanity, the still unravished bride of all that's dashing, yet handy with the pertness of Cockaigne. The Baron must be the very spectre of poverty, the Dame lachrymose as a relict, yet endowed with potential skittishness. The Ugly Sisters are to declare the irrevocable male, the Babes remain sexless as Cherub and Seraph, unemergent from pure angelhood. These things are part of the Butlerian philosophy of Unconscious Memory, and are not lightly to be denied. Not even Mr. Cochran may play tricks with heredity. A hundred years hence, when parents have really cottoned to Russian ballet, the minds of their children may have become artistic. But let us not pretend that that time is here.

Babes in the Wood is a compromise between the

Any Child's Play

traditional and the new-fangled. The story is of an admirable expectedness until a Maeterlinckian spell turns the children into adolescents, when, of course, they lose interest. The dialogue is capital; there is not a joke beyond childish grasp. There is not even a mention of the modern Bluebeard. Like that matrimonially inclined Frenchwoman who advertised in a catalogue of her charms *pas de piano*, Mr. Cochran might justifiably notify parents *pas de Landru*. It is the setting which gives me pause. "On the Edge of the Wood" would make a charming poster for the Underground; only the details of the route are lacking. "The Dream Nursery" could go straight into *Petrouchka*, and "Where the Toys Come From" into *La Boutique Fantasque*. Will children, I wonder, recognize these things as glorifications of the familiar, and will they accept the hardly seen, luminous moths of M. Poiret in place of real robins with practicable beaks and tail-feathers? "The Interior of the Castle," an austerity in stained glass, is altogether contrary to my recollection of a grand finale or "Palace Scene." This is no palace, but a profiteer's shooting-box. One knows these flunkeys; they were obtained through the "Morning Post" and "strongly recommended by Lord X who is going abroad." I am uneasy, too, about the dancing. Any right-minded child would, of a certainty, give all the dancing-masters in Russia for Mr. John Tiller. There should be as much "dressing" about the ballet as about a parade of toy-soldiers set out upon the nursery floor. Mr. Cochran's troops deploy in unadmired disorder, and those ignorant of the higher functions of the ballet might deem this not to be dancing.

Any Child's Play

Robin Hood is admittedly the least grateful of all
" principal boy " parts.   Not for him the jewelled
whip and garter, the three-cornered hat, the *jabot* with
the single diamond, the poise of Brummel turned
Sixteen-string Jack.   He is no highwayman of the passions with a commanding trick of the heel, but a simple
woodlander, an amorous bumpkin.   Rather, for him,
the green thought in the green shade.   But your true
" principal boy " is not concerned with verisimilitude.
There is, alas! not one ounce of thigh-slapping in Miss
Nellie Taylor's elegant ruffian, whose love-making has
none of that quality which is properly called " spank-
ing."   He never drove a coach-and-four through a
crowded card-room at midnight.   How would a Harriet
Vernon have scorned those blameless " trunks," sage
in colour and implication, circumfluent as the hose of
Madge Robertson's, now Mrs. Kendal's, Rosalind!
Mr. George Hassell and Mr. Tubby Edlin hardly give
one the impression, as the Brothers Griffiths used to do,
of having lived for an eternity in each other's bosoms.
Mr. Hassell is too obviously the master-mind.   Both
villains should be double-dyed till put to the proof; Mr.
Edlin's knees are as water from the start.   Mr. A. W.
Baskcomb's Louise is a sheer delight.   Her mien that
of the lamentable Miss Jones arriving to take charge of
Mr. Walpole's " Jeremy," she wears the classic air of
dejection proper to governesses, an air primarily of
the desire to please recurrent with each new place, but
with a subtle layer of heaped-up humiliation.   One
visualizes angry middle-class debates in which the
privilege of dining with the family is conceded, on
Sundays, at midday.   When, later, Louise burgeons to

recovered beauty and puts out fresh leaves, you note that she still retains her mittens. This is the stroke of an artist.

I have left the Babes to the last. "Complementary colours," says a text-book on astronomy, "are not uncommon among double stars, the brighter usually having a red, orange, or yellow colour, the less bright a green, blue, or purple." This law holds true of the stage. Lorna's impeccable *tenue* is the charter for the eccentricities of Toots; Beattie's constant gentility the excuse for the excesses of Babs. I declare Miss Jenny Dolly to shine with an orange light, Miss Rosie to send forth a blue. From the boy-babe's pathetic countenance, composed after the model of Sarah's Jeanne d'Arc, there issues a constant stream of pleasant-sounding Amurricanisms. The girl-babe is self-effacing, the perfect Celia. Both, one feels, are thoroughly capable women. But their legs should be covered. There is no beauty, save that of efficiency, in the musculature, the ligaments and articulations of practised dancers. There was an unfortunate mishap on the night on which I attended; a back-cloth refused to descend and remained a foot from the ground. Urgently the feet of the scene-shifters like desperate mice peeped in and out, but without avail. Meanwhile, with cloudy brow, Mr. Cochran sate sepulchral in his box. Presently to the clod-hopping soles was added a nattier pair, but ever, and to the end of the scene, in vain. Happy Mr. Cochran that pantomime is a world as yet by him unconquered! I do not refer to this simple hitch, but to the whole conception. *Babes in the Wood* is a pantomime for grown-ups. " Tout genre a son écueil

Any Child's Play

particulier," said Sainte-Beuve. The rock on which this
" children's pantomime " has split is Chauve-Souris.
Mr. Cochran has not been sufficiently 'ware of M.
Nikita Balieff.

Some Foreign Plays

Thérèse Raquin, by Emile Zola. Brixton Theatre.
Jacqueline, by Sacha Guitry. Princes Theatre.
Uncle Vanya, by Tchehov. Everyman Theatre.

THERESE RAQUIN IS THE LAST ITEM in the admirable programme presented at the Brixton Theatre by the Birmingham Repertory Company. I am not going to say that Zola's exacting drama was adequately acted; but better, it seems to me, an honest failure to achieve a big thing than the competent bringing off of rubbish. Let me admit that the acting at Brixton was middling. Yet I claim for it that it was full of interest. You rushed, if you had the root of appreciation in you, to the help of players who so obviously possessed the root of intention; theirs were straits in which it was your plain duty to throw the lifeline of intelligent sympathy.

The author of this piece, a writer now deemed old-fashioned, was a revolutionary fellow in his day. Ten years before Zola was born Victor Hugo had blown in the windows of the classic theatre with his great gust of romance. When Zola was twenty-five the Goncourts, secretly holding romance to be fustian and Hugo a giant grown musty, bundled both out of the theatre with *Henriette Maréchal*. At the age of thirty-three Zola out-naturalized the naturalists with a study of the working classes of Paris, whose passions and crimes he declared

174

to be pure animal appetites and expedients. Conscience they knew not; remorse was pathological, a derangement of the nervous system. In this novel he supposes a marriage between Thérèse, the adopted daughter of a small shopkeeper, and a weakling son, Camille. At unattractive length he insists upon the full-bloodedness of Thérèse and the indolence of her husband. Apart from two retired functionaries, ridiculous and wearisome, the *ménage* has no visitors except a railway employé with broad shoulders, the neck of a bull, hands to fell an ox, and a mediocre talent for drawing. The quality of physical clumsiness, which in Charles Bovary was so displeasing to Emma, enchants Thérèse. She becomes the mistress of Laurent, who is ravished to find an inexpensive leman. There is no stint of infamy. Laurent is as cowardly as he is mean. Prudence and not jealousy is the motive which prompts him to murder the husband. He has no love for Thérèse, only some habit of the senses. Freudians and old-fashioned moralists will delight to note the tangle Zola got himself into after the murder with his autopsical pretensions, his self-elected presidency of a court of crowner's quest having purely material terms of reference. Suffering the pangs not of remorse but of nervous derangement, Laurent becomes an artist of finer calibre. Unfortunately his portraits have acquired the, we must presume, pathological trick of looking like the dead man. He cannot sleep. Laurent hath murdered sleep. Thérèse repulses him on their wedding night; the lovers have murdered passion. Together they start at ghosts, of sorriest fancies their companions making. Old Madame Raquin being now stricken with paralysis,

175

her daughter and son-in-law indulge their recriminations before her eyes, the only part of her which still lives. Once her hand comes to life and in the presence of the stupid functionaries traces on the table-cloth the beginning of a denunciation. But paralysis again supervenes. Finally, after attempts at mutual destruction, husband and wife decide that it is better to die than on the torture of a deranged nervous system to lie in ecstasy. Decidedly the play begins to look like *Macbeth*, and that, we know, was no tale of mere animals. The truth is that Zola's "pure animalism" is sheer fudge.

In the theatre Zola recognized this. In his stage version of the novel he eliminated the brute and turned Laurent into an ardent, well set-up young lover, endowed with what the French call *fougue*, a quality considered by them as not ignoble. Taxed, Zola might have pleaded that it was not possible to put Charles Bovary on the stage; that Rodolphe was more practicable. But Zola in those days was never taxed with anything more subtle than the ambition to stand with Flaubert before the Tribunal Correctionnel. His real offence was that in transcribing for the theatre he wilfully committed that falsification of values repugnant to the sincere artist. This particular falsification was probably essential to stage performance of the play. Minor alterations were immaterial. By all means let the husband on the night of his wedding destroy the portrait of Camille. "Thou hast no speculation in those eyes," he shouts, or words to that effect, overhearing which Madame Raquin, who has entered inopportunely, has her seizure. It is immaterial that the old woman should wilfully ſtop in the middle of her denunciation so as to prolong the evildoers' torment, that she should wake from her torpor to propel the knife towards Thérèse, that she should, at the end, give tongue like an Avenging Angel. These things in the theatre are good. Good, too, is the taking up of the act-drop a year after the murder, with all but one of the characters drawing up their chairs to the same routine of dominoes upon which the curtain had fallen at the end of the firſt scene with the murder juſt mooted. This is good ſtage-craft and the proper business of the theatre. The moral of the book in its firſt half is that wolves and butchers muſt have nerves to ſtand the bleating of ghoſtly sheep; in its second that the modern Ægiſthus and Clytemneſtra muſt expect as thin a time as their forbears experienced after the murder of Agamemnon. This is a contradiction. The moral of the play is the whole-hearted one that the wages of sin is the inability to enjoy the fruits of sin. The piece was well worth reviving. Conceiving it his duty to proteſt againſt the Romantics with their glorified ſtories of changelings, their windy nursery-moralities and their *grands mots bêtes*—Hugo himself was not free from a kind of mouthing silliness—the proteſter went too far for common sense and not far enough for high tragedy. What Zola's play lacks is nobility. But nobility to this realiſt was *vieux jeu*, the worn-out fashion of Æschylus and Shakespeare, Racine, *le père* Hugo, the whole bombaſtic crowd. Ignobility was his theme, the bee in a very clever bonnet.

The play undeniably provides three great rôles for actors who can inspire awe. Miss Aida Jenoure made a very brave shot at the part in which Marie Laurent was said to be really terrifying. To blow the trumpet of the Day of Judgment is probably beyond the power of any living English actress, but Miss Jenoure found a good intonation for the final " They have died too soon." The part of Thérèse is laid out for an actress with a greater variety of emotional power than Miss Margaret Chatwin possesses. If and when Miss Thorndike tires of snippet atrocity, she might try this full-length fall, though she would be better as Clytemnestra. I can think of no other fashionable London actress, except Miss Ethel Irving, who could get near the animalism of the part. Here Miss Chatwin had a kind of brute sincerity which was as successful, perhaps, as a more nicely-perfected art. If Mr. Leslie Banks could transfer himself to the heavyweight division he would be a perfect Laurent. His American soldier showed that he has the blend of ferocity and meanness that the part demands. Mr. Grosvenor North endowed it with a mild eye, gentle manners, and an attractive, melancholy beard. But I respected his performance and some even less successful ones for their obvious sincerity and good intent.

Grounded on the admirable Mrs. Fawcett, I long revered political economy as an exact science, all mouthing human passion far above. Rude was the awakening. Orators with burning foreheads and with parching tongues—hence the water-bottle before them—waved a big loaf and a little, asseverating that but for the purblind the labourer should acquire the one as cheaply as the other. To which the acidulated retort that half a

178

Some Foreign Plays

loaf is better than no bread. Or they vociferated that a tax on American wheat (*a*) would keep it out to the benefit of the home grower, or (*b*) let it in to the reduction of the National Debt, whilst anyway, (*c*) America would pay our tax. Childhood's mentor had treated these things as matters of reasoning; these noisy polemics were all for passion. Then when I applied me to the artist-thinker, Mr. Shaw or another, to ask how these things might be reconciled, it was to learn that politicians were knaves whose bellies were better unfilled.

Still I must hold that each country can benefit its neighbour, and that reciprocal taxation is nonsense. I do not believe that our Château Bermondsey of the year before last will ever be the equal of the Léoville Barton of '78, or that our Bass is not better than the miserable Bock of the boulevards. Why not a free exchange ? Why not send cricket bats to Cuba in return for cigars ? Why not import French actors and export our players of Association football ? Let it be supposed that, following representations from the Actors' Trades Union the Government had imposed a tax preventive or admissive of those great artists, the Guitrys, and in the certainty that the French would pay. It seems to me, that only if enough English playgoers had been found to afford the increased price of the seats, would the visit have run its course. In no case do I see the Parisian paying for the Londoner. What is certain is that the absence of a prohibitory tax did no harm to the English actor, the audience at the Princes Theatre obviously not being drawn from other playhouses. It was a re-creation of the old pre-war assemblage of cultivated persons, whose intelligence the post-war theatre offends. Conversely

179

Some Foreign Plays

the imposition of a tax would not have benefited the English actor. When the price of Havana cigars becomes prohibitive your connoisseur does not decline upon the British. He abstains. This cultivated audience cannot be imagined flocking in the alternative to *Miss Babbs from Babbicombe*, or *Have you the Ready?*

French heroic acting is not essentially better than English. To Talma we can oppose Kean, to Lemaître, Kemble. It is true that in the matter of *tragédiennes* they are " one up." Our Sarah cancelling theirs, Rachel remains over. But since Bernhardt and her predecessor belong less to France than to the commonwealth of the Jews we need not be discomfited. Among modern comparisons Mounet-Sully was not greater than Irving, and Réjane did not outshine our own dear lady. The English Sans-Gêne was bad; the Frenchwoman had the wit to leave Beatrice alone. Guitry *père* is a great actor and his husband in *Jacqueline* is a fine performance. But let me produce Mr. Edmund Gwenn in a transposition of the part—and my producing shall mean no other than a hint to play less to eye and ear and more to the imagination—and I promise that you shall not be ashamed. Sacha has done nothing comparable to the latest performance of Mr. Seymour Hicks. Mdlle. Yvonne Printemps? Here I confess a check. Beauty, charm, verve, a capacity for *gaminerie* and pathos, a natural sparkle allied to immense technical accomplishment—genius, in a word—these things do not easily find their parallel. It is in the non-heroic drama that the French have a pull, and for an obvious reason. The essence of English acting is the suggestion of emotion reserved; you would recognize it by the wall it builds round passion. The French use restraint only to heighten the effect when, ultimately, they burst the dam. Our best brains, condescending to the theatre, treat passionately of every subject save the one upon which French playwrights harp incessantly. The preoccupations of a Shaw, a Galsworthy, or a Barker are nothing to the French dramatists, Brieux excepted. *L'Amour*! they cry, and ring up the curtain exactly where Dumas let it fall on his sentimental *cocotte* three-quarters of a century ago. This chatter of pure love proceeds out of the mouth of your French actor as naturally as *bel canto* out of the throat of an Italian opera singer. He knows that his familiar tornado, spouting from his withered cheeks anew, will sweep his Latin audience off its feet as surely as the top note of the garlic-eating Marseilles tenor. And so we get such a scene as that incredible third act of *Jacqueline*. Jacqueline has been shot by her lover's outraged wife, who now comes to Jacqueline's husband to bemire the dead woman's memory and to offer to take her place. Now what does your well-bred English actor do in like circumstance? What would the General in *Loyalties* do? The muscles twitch in Mr. Dawson Milward's cheek, hard bites he on his cigar— no, he would not be smoking—with clenched hands he advances, halts, and rings for his servant to turn the woman out. As an Englishman I admire Mr. Milward's acting immensely; as a Frenchman I should not consider it acting at all. Mark, now, what Guitry does. " Vous osez me parler de Jacqueline! " he says, quietly, but with a tremendous groundswell. When the woman would by repetition profane Jacqueline's last words, he stops her mouth. Then, with all the fineness of the logical French mind and much forensic shaking of the forefinger, he drags from this unwilling witness the basest of her thought. The violent purging of that opposing bosom rouses the Sadist for whom we have been prepared. With his hands round her throat he demands to hear Jacqueline's last words. "Elle me demandait pardon," gasps the wanton and tightens her executioner's grasp. In the portrayal of passion we cannot rival the French. They are our masters, too, in the presentation of the pathetic in comic envelope. What English actor could give the friend in *Jacqueline* as M. Berthier presents him ? This shrinking affronter of destiny, whose thin hair, non-committal beard, and irresolute, sagging paunch bespeak so little of valiance, confronting that domineering other, expands into life itself and yet remains comic. This leaves us silent. But here French supremacy ends, if you except that knack of quick speech and the happy casualness with which they plunge into importancy without the orchestral *apéritif*, that English exordium to long-windedness. In three hours they will dispose of a full-length play and throw in *Le Misanthrope*! No waiting on the expected, that torture of the damned.

Tchehov's *Uncle Vanya* is an embroidery upon the theme of apprenticeship to sorrow: "Nous sommes les apprentis, la douleur est notre maître." It is a theme which no age or country escapes. Musset may sing it after one fashion, Shakespeare after another. Yet it has been known to cause the practical mind to suffer impatience when it comprehends that Tchehov's sorrowful apprentices are *fainéants*. Vanya, the senti-

mentalist, unpacks his heart with words, nags at the
fate he will not unbend his idealistic soul to conquer.
Astrov, the man of action, gives his life to drunkenness
and the cultivation of trees. Serebryakov, the invalid,
is pure humbug. His wife Elena, loving Astrov, lacks
the courage of adultery; she is in no sense moral. Sonia,
his daughter, loving Astrov, is a sick lily. We watch
these people curiously, but without comprehension and
almost without pity. They are, oh, so exasperatingly
Russian! " At last," says Stevenson of the death of
Bragelonne, " the little Viscount has done something.
C'est, ma foi! bien heureux." But these Tchehovians
do nothing. C'est ma foi! bien malheureux. They do
not even commit suicide, and when they shoot to kill
they miss. They make up that most helpless of cor-
porations, the spineless introspective. They do not
indulge in that last Western consolation: " No dog so
wretched but he wags his tail sometimes." We English
have few wounds which a ride to hounds will not heal.
Your Russian, we are always told, is a great huntsman.
But these characters of Tchehov do not hunt; they are
hunted. The ideal pursues them, flays them with a
whip.

I am as certain that this play of castigation is a masterpiece as I am that I shall never get into touch with
the whipped. Who to me says Russian says Czecho-
Slovakian, Magyar, Turk. A witty French lady once
declared that she drew her line at Lucerne. East of
that line, " ce sont des crocodiles." (Have not the tears
of that species been observed as far West as Geneva ?)
The books do not help one very much. I read that
" To the Russian European culture and ethic is a virus,

working in him like a disease of which the inflammation comes forth as literature. Since Peter the Great Russia has been accepting Europe, and seething Europe down in a curious process of katabolism." I look this word up, to find that it means "Destructive or downward metabolism; retrogressive metamorphism—opposed to *anabolism*. See DISASSIMILATION." But I will not pursue the dictionary further. Scratch your Tchehovian and you find a crocodile, is enough for me. As a play *Uncle Vanya* is quite perfect. I shall never know exactly "what it means," but then I do not know that I hunger for that knowledge. It is, and that suffices. It was acted with infinite tenderness and susceptibility by that sensitive player, Mr. Leon Quartermaine, with veracity and humour by that tremendous Iago-in-waiting, Mr. Franklin Dyall. As Serebryakov Mr. Hignett was quite pointedly miscast. There is not, nor ever can be, an ounce of humbug in the composition of this charming actor. Miss Cathleen Nesbitt gave very exactly the impression of demanding more from life than it can reasonably hold. She divided Elena accurately into two compatible halves, self-absorption and self-sacrifice. Miss Irene Rathbone, the helpless lily among weeds, just managed to keep her head above water. But my special admiration is reserved for the Telyegen of Mr. Joseph A. Dodd.* Here is unquestioning acceptance of destiny, the only safe shelter from

---

* This actor has died since the above was written. In recent years he played three parts in London which aroused the greatest admiration. Telyegen, Foldal in *John Gabriel Borkman*, and the negro in *Abraham Lincoln*. He was an actor of exquisite finish who was quite insufficiently appreciated.

life. Alone of all the characters he keeps humility between him and the myriad universes of the night. " Bless in me "—it is Loti's little steeple which speaks— " the shield which guards you from the abyss. Seek, in your infinite littleness, to emulate the dead sleeping at my feet, who departed in simple faith, unmindful of the void and without trouble of the stars." For Tely-egen alone of these unquiet Russians there is blessed unquestioning. He keeps his face to earth.

The Cenci

The Cenci, by Percy Bysshe Shelley.   New Theatre.

HE PURITANICAL KINK IN THE English character has been responsible for many strange things, but for nothing stranger than the insistence upon the fusion of art and morality. A bowing acquaintance, a loosely woven *liaison*, are not enough; nothing short of complete and irremediable marriage will do.   The first thing our good Puritans demand to know about a work of art is not whether it is beautiful or true, but whether it urges the spectator to do a good thing or to refrain from a bad one. With this proviso, that if the bad thing is dark, violent, and abhorrent, it were more moral to leave ill alone and bid the artist keep silent.   For exactly one hundred and three years the Puritans have stopped the mouth of one of the greatest of English singers. As gullible as they are fearful, they have found no difficulty in believing not only that a play founded upon an immoral act must necessarily be immoral, but also that Shelley could bend his glorious mind to the exploitation of immorality. The silliness still persists.   Recently a newspaper informed its million readers that, the Censor having removed his predecessors' ban, Miss Sybil Thorndike would, at the New Theatre, produce Shelley's " dull and dirty " play.

The point about *The Cenci* is that it is not only not a

The Cenci

play about incest, but that it is more than a " play."
It is, strictly speaking, a " morality," an exhortation,
part of the passionate propaganda of a noble mind,
which swells the theatre of its presentation to the scope
and dimension of a cathedral. Unless the spectator
condone and co-operate in this noble misuse of the playhouse, he is in danger of thinking that perhaps the
censors were not so very wrong after all, that the moral
hardly atones for the vicious display. Shelley himself
is largely to blame. We find him writing: " *The
Cenci* is a work of art; it is not coloured by my feel-
ings nor obscured by my metaphysics." This is an
old tale—genius pretending its work to be that of the
plain man. So Ibsen thought; so, probably, thinks Mr.
Shaw. Whereas genius must ever write more preg-
nantly than it knows. Shelley could not set down " A
cat is on a mat " without giving puss a metaphysical
turn. *The Cenci* is written on three planes—a ground-
floor of normal significance, a middle storey of spiritual
meaning, and an attic wherein the idea streams out of
window, the emanation of a philosophy.

When I entered the theatre my recollection of the
play was of the haziest. Before the end of the first scene
I realized that I was not to feel pity for the man, nor
terror at his example, who was the prey of unlawful
passion. Cenci proclaimed himself outside all lusts
save that of cruelty, a case not for the artist, but the
alienist. It seemed, for an act or so, that the thing was
not quite worth while, that it hardly needed a Shelley to
put together this tale of injury, vengeance, and the law's
insensible machinery. So far the theatre remained the
theatre. One could admire Miss Thorndike's admir-

187

ably collected beginning and her crescendo of nerves.
One had time to admire the colour and grouping of the
scenes. Cenci dispatched, a new spirit at once disen-
gaged itself. The motive changed from incest to parri-
cide, and what I have called the second storey of spiritual
significance became apparent in Miss Thorndike's
idealized figure of Injury and in the justiciary's identifi-
cation of her deed of murder with that of rebellion
against the paternal authority of the Church. One felt
that if Beatrice had been the chief figure in a non-
metaphysical tragedy she would have trumpeted her
guilt and proclaimed it innocence. Here she was, however, equivocating like a Greek and lying like a Trojan,
fighting authority with its own weapons. Subtle as any
casuist, and since to her this killing was no murder,
she swore roundly that she had no hand in it. More
than ever was Miss Thorndike the play here. First
she had been an individual victim, then a symbol of
maiden virtue rudely strumpeted, and now she rose to
the embodiment of a pure philosophic idea—the idea of
Rebellion. This was what Shelley, whose ruling passion was revolt, was after. He had filled his play with
pretty phrases else, whereas in the matter of poetry
he had actually kept it as " dry " as an American
saloon. Great poets are not abstemious to no purpose. Shelley began apparently with the idea of a
darkly fascinating play on the lines of Cyril Tourneur,
but the demon or apostle of revolt soon pushed the mere
playwright from his stool. Miss Thorndike made this
perfectly obvious from the impersonal quality of the
later scenes. Beatrice was, as it were, *distraite*, her
mind obviously elsewhere, in the attic with the dreamer.

The Cenci

If you insist that I must declare what, exactly, they were both in revolt about—well, there you 'ave me, as the chauffeur in Mr. Harwood's play remarked. But the business of a rebel is to rebel—it would not seem to matter much to what end. Shelley passed through the world like a torch, equal parts of smoke and flame. And a torch is doubtless " a fine thing under guidance—under guidance you know," as George Eliot's Mr. Brooke said of Ladislaw's enthusiasm when he compared it with our poet's.

Shelley's revolutionary zeal could find fuel everywhere. Mr. Marion Crawford, in a careful survey of the evidence, came to the conclusion that both Cenci and the Pope were much maligned in the popular version of the story and that Beatrice, finding herself with child of an unconfessed amour and murdering her father for fear of discovery, was justly condemned. It is a moot point whether Shelley would not have been furious at the new evidence, since it would have robbed him of the thing nearest his heart—a grievance to be shrieked to Heaven. And the old story, even if it were a lying one, was a good enough stick for the belabouring of authority.

I shall say no more of Miss Thorndike, save that she was the architect of my three-storeyed house. This is no high faluting pretence; the least expert playgoer must have shared my edification. Mr. Robert Farquharson's Count did not impress me. With great lack of discretion his performance had been heralded by the paragraphists as the greatest thing in tragic acting on the English stage. A young actor from Italy would, meteor-like, flash into our ken and prove,

The Cenci

as his Herod proved, etc., etc. I feel sure that Mr.
Farquharson resents this puffery. He is too much of
an artist not to realize that great actors are not made
out of occasional portraits of decadent senility. Fortunately, he has some other performances of a different
order in beauty to his credit; what he lacks now, to become a really fine actor, is the continual traffic of the
stage. His Count seemed to me a lath painted to look
like horror; at times a chubby, almost boyish countenance peeped disconcertingly out. The actor over-
mouthed his words, pulling his jowl as though he would
put the whole of hell into each single phrase. Being
overdone, the evil was less than implacable; you felt
that it was painted on the cheek, not that it came from
the soul. These, you whispered your neighbour, were
the faces that Quilp made to intimidate his spouse.
The voice, too, was light in quality, and before the
final curse was reached conviction was spent. Nevertheless, the performance was obviously informed with
intelligence, but to claim for it the highest degree
of tragic, or even horrific, passion is to forget Irving.
Mr. Lawrence Anderson's Giacomo was distinguished,
Mr. Casson's Judge finely inappeasable, and there was
magnificent acting in Mr. Victor Lewisohn's Margio.
As a display of power and reality this has haunted me.
But I come back to Sybil. She was not pathetic, but
then, to my mind, Sybil never is pathetic. Perhaps it
would be more fair if I were to confess that there is
something in me which refuses to be stirred emotion-
ally by this actress. Sybil has only to come on to the
stage and I am at once antagonistic. I want to pit my
brain against hers; I resent having to take that intellect,

190

as it were, sitting down. In other words, her acting seems to me to be hard—hard as nails. There is too much firmness about those lips which, when they droop, droop to malice. I should as soon think of being sorry for a marble statue as of being sorry for Sybil. In plays like *The Cenci* this hardness has extraordinary value: it allows you to see through it to the play. What a mess Sarah would have made of it! Let her loose on that scene of execution, and you would have beheld nothing at all of Shelley's play, and the actual stage only through a mist of tears. But whether the figure now about to have its head cut off was Beatrice or Marie Antoinette you would have neither known nor cared. There is something here other than the question of a greater or lesser artist. There are, I suppose, some three thousand ways in which Sarah is a more accomplished actress than Sybil, ways of which the English artist must have perception since she tries to bring the same things off herself. But there is one matter in which Sybil not only beats her great rival, but is so immeasurably her superior that she disappears from view—that matter being the conveyance of moral grandeur. "Ah ça!" I can imagine Sarah saying, "ce n'est pas mon affaire!" And, of course, that particular quality is not Sarah's business, while it is, very definitely, Sybil's.

In the Pit

HE LAUGHING LADY IS A DELIGHT-ful comedy.   That is to say, I found manifold delight in it, standing at the back of the pit at the Globe Theatre in uncomfortable proximity to an apparatus for overheating.   It was the fault of the skipping hills above Windermere that I overlooked Mr. Sutro's first night.   I had played wretched golf.   My eye, scorning the diminutive, dimpled globe resting on the tee, would wander to the many-coloured waters spread out beneath.   Obedient to higher rule my head would ever and anon lift itself to the eternal hills.   In short, I could not keep my eye on the ball. But neither could I keep my eye on the London theatre; and this first night slipped away unattended by me. The management was all forbearance and courtesy, but regretted that it had not a vacant seat for my first afternoon in town.   Where there's a will there's a three-shilling way, and that sum I cheerfully disbursed the following Saturday for the privilege of being the last person to squeeze into the pit.

One has often descanted vaguely upon the corporate entity of theatre audiences.   I now know that this thing exists.   I know for a certainty that those of us who stood upon each others' toes that afternoon were collectively one—one in our efforts to get away from the over-

In the Pit

enthusiastic radiator and behind someone shorter than
one's self, one in offering each other a share of the hired
opera-glasses, one in discussing in the intervals, sitting
out on the cold and draughty steps leading down from
the street into the pit, how the play would or should end.
I imagine that few of us knew what upsetting a dinner-
table meant except in the literal sense, or could measure
the exact depth of Mrs. Playgate's perturbation on
learning that her husband (Mr. Herbert Ross) had
acceded to the proposal of that afternoon's *divorcée* that
she should join them at dinner. For we, in our serried
ranks, at our grossest live that we may eat; Mrs. Playgate (Miss Henrietta Watson) lives that she may dine
other people smartly, an existence not only pointless,
but perilous—life on the edge of a precipice, where a
single slip means social extinction. Mr. Playgate's
gaffe was, indeed, enormous. For the other guests
included the multi-millionaire, Sir Harrison Peters,
K.B.E., the viperine Cynthia Dell, the great Daniel Farr,
K.C., who, a few hours earlier, had put Lady Marjorie
" through " it, leaving her " without a shred," and Mrs.
Farr, his helpmeet. Playgate had indeed gone over the
edge. Mrs. Playgate stuck her heels in earth and be-
layed the rope round the butler, whom she bade lay
another place and hand the following note to Lady
Marjorie upon arrival: " My dear Marjorie; Mr. Farr
is dining here to-night. Caroline." And then the
guests began to arrive. First the millionaire (Mr. Julian
Royce) very spruce and dapper. Then Cynthia Dell
(Miss Edith Evans). Next, Daniel Farr, K.C. (Mr.
Godfrey Tearle), glum as Othello when the poison begins
to work, and Mrs. Farr (Miss Violet Vanbrugh) in

symbolical black. Finally, undeterred, Lady Marjorie
(Miss Marie Löhr) enters, in a confection positively
bridal. Madame is not served until after such interval
as allows the scapegrace to make explanation of the mis-
understandings which have culminated in divorce. Her
ladyship had merely wished to teach the neglectful Sir
Hector Colladine, Bart., D.S.O., a lesson. He, poor
fellow, having been educated at Eton, naturally found
letter-writing a strain. The Himalayas making a man
jealous, Sir Hector believed the worst when the gossips
wrote to say that some little whipper-snapper had been
surprised at Lady Marjorie's in his pyjamas. (" Only
in her sitting-room," urges honest Playgate. " Darling,"
gurgles Cynthia, " I love you for that! ") We know,
of course, that Lady Marjorie is innocent, or she would
not wear the lineaments of Miss Marie Löhr; what we
are to learn is that she would have allowed the suit to go
undefended, but for the child who, she finds, is dear to
her. At this point a few tears trickle unconvincingly
down Marjorie's innocent nose. Though the recital
has not varied one tittle from the tale told in the box,
the K.C. now as implicitly believes its truth as, a few
hours earlier, he explicitly denied it. Mrs. Playgate's
party is saved; counsel and victim get on together like
a house on fire. As they troop into dinner somebody
says: " Oh, Marjorie, as for that little matter of social
ostracism "—in these exalted circles people are not
merely cut—" you may be thankful you are not plain
Mrs. Smith of Peckham." At these harmless words the
dumpy little woman in front of me, over whose nonsensical bonnet I had glimpsed the absurdities of Mayfair, gave a palpable start. At this point the curtain is

lowered for a moment. When it is raised again the ladies are re-entering the drawing-room to smoke. You, dear reader and expert playgoer, know without being told what has happened. We, in the pit, knew that one thing only could have happened; yet despite that knowledge we were actually and metaphorically on tiptoe to see and hear it expounded. The scene, you see, had been well prepared by a competent playwright, and competence in play-making means no more than the ability to tell once again, and amusingly, the hundred-times told tale. In short, Farr had fallen in love with Marjorie.

Now there were all the elements of serious discussion here. What is Mrs. Farr to do when she discovers that the man whom she has nursed into fame and to whom she has borne children is prepared to throw over fame, wife, and all the honourable rest of it " for a pretty face " ? That, I think, is the consecrated and belittling phrase used by people who look with disinterested eye upon the sudden distemper of the married man. Writers of all kinds have been prodigal of nostrums—quack remedies for the reconciliation of happiness and morality. Stevenson turned the difficulty by means of pretty phrases—spring, you remember, was to sow riot in the blood and passing faces leave passing regrets. R. L. S. would have prescribed *for the husband*—a week at St. Andrew's or a tour of the Highlands. Mrs. W. K. Clifford thought that the proper thing was for the wife to throw herself overboard a channel steamer. Sir Arthur Pinero would doubtless proffer the husband Hilary Jesson's " halo of renunciation." Balzac devotes a whole book to pointing out that in these cases

In the Pit

it comes devilish expensive for the man. *A combien l'amour revient aux vieillards* is to be found on the fly-leaf of, I think, the second volume of " Splendeurs et Misères des Courtisanes." Bataille makes magnificent play with the situation in *La Vierge Folle*. This was the last play in which I saw Réjane, and I shall never forget how she sat on her husband's trunk and, for the better part of an hour, dissolved the house in tears. The French wife steadfastly refused to divorce her husband, insisting that he should go away with the ninny and return to her in the day of weariness. Mr. St. John Ervine shows Jane Clegg acquiescing in complete abandonment. Much depends upon the kind of person the wife is, upon the kind of playwright her creator is, and the kind of theatre for which he writes. Mr. Sutro does, indeed, make Mrs. Farr suggest to Marjorie that they should agree upon some working compromise, the essence of which is that the mistress shall enjoy her husband for a time, and return him as little damaged as possible. The play taking place at the Globe Theatre, and Miss Löhr enacting Marjorie, it is obvious that the project has only to be hinted to be scouted. (It was a feasible proposal inasmuch as Farr had enough money for the two establishments. Ibsen would have begun his play three years after the arrangement had been in working order.) The *clou* to *The Laughing Lady*, it begins to be apparent, is her enactress. Any serious view of the situation—whether we see through the eyes of Bataille, Ervine, or Mrs. Clifford—at once seizes upon the wife as the important figure, the one person in whom the drama centres. The mistress may be anybody. Now this, we may be sure, would not in the

In the Pit

least suit Miss Löhr who, in her own theatre, is obviously not anybody, but a very important somebody. The play, then, must centre in Marjorie; and centering in that young lady, it resolves itself into a discussion as remote from human life as if the characters lived on another planet. But this, in the pit, is quite as it should be. To us Mayfair is another planet. I would not have missed a word of what followed, artificial though it all was.

I would not have missed the millionaire's offer to Lady Marjorie of a flat, a motor-car, and £10,000. I would not, for anything, have missed my dumpy little woman's audible gulp at the mention of the round sum. " Quand il n'y en aura plus, il y en aura encore," said Gaston Rieux in the old play, when he put the twenty-five louis into the drawer in Marguerite's dressing-table. " When the ten thousand pounds are spent, there'll be another ten thousand," said the magnificent fellow, and my little woman gave yet another gulp. I would not have missed the divorcing, yet doting, husband (Mr. Brian Gilmour), who returns from his Mount Everest expedition just in time to kick the millionaire out with that expedition's thickest boot. Nor the zest with which, in favour of the lady, the K.C. proposes to abandon wife, children, and career. Nor the unction with which he denounces as a despicable hound the poor millionaire who isn't going to abandon anybody. Nor Lady Marjorie's outraged airs, nor yet the K.C.'s enforced virtuous graces. I repeat, I wouldn't have missed a word of it. To be back in a London pit watching these funny little creatures plash about on the surface of life and reveal nothing of its depths, was

197

In the Pit

better fun than playing bad golf at Windermere. It was only when, at the long last, the curtain fell on the beatific vision of Sir Hector clasping Lady Marjorie to his public-school bosom that I realized how tired I was of standing, of the indefatigable radiator, and of dumpy Mrs. Smith from Peckham.

It was the acting which had beguiled tedium. Not, let me say, the acting of Miss Marie Löhr, though that was pleasant enough. There is nothing " in " Lady Marjorie, and her enactress put her on the stage with rippling ease. Nor yet the acting of Miss Henrietta Watson, whom I liked all the better for her failure to suggest the absurd hostess. How, indeed, could she suggest her ? There is enough common sense in this clever actress's little finger to flay all the Mrs. Playgates in London. Nor yet that of Miss Violet Vanbrugh who, nevertheless, made a fine show of dignity in the play's one approach to sincerity. And I do not think I could have supported many more speeches from Mr. Godfrey Tearle. " There is something ridiculous about a husband," said Vronsky, in " Anna Karenina," and Balzac certainly saw the fun in Nucingen, whose passionate declaration to Esther Gobseck, " Cheu fous atore ! "—a declaration torn from the very heart of his money-bags—ranks among the great comic pronouncements. Mr. Tearle is above all things a serious actor, one in whom I have never been able to detect the smallest glint of comic perception. Nucingen, at his most inflamed, was conscious of the grotesque richness of the spectacle which his passion presented to the world. Mr. Tearle threw over his ardours the sanctity of a rite : he was faintly sanctimonious. I do not imagine that it

In the Pit

is in the actor's power to correct this; Forbes-Robertson in a morning coat was ever sanctimonious. Mr. Tearle's personality is altogether too romantic for morning coats, telephones, and other mundanities. He is a fine actor who needs a toga and lashings of blank verse.

The performance which enchanted me was that of Miss Edith Evans. Miss Evans is the most brilliant and accomplished of English actresses. She may not have Miss Thorndike's power, but she has compensating pathos—witness her *dévote* in *Les Trois Filles de M. Dupont* and her housemaid in *I Serve*—a positively scarifying amount of brains, and an unrivalled comic instinct. Her Cleopatra in Dryden's *All for Love* was a Lely of exquisite distinction; her Cynthia is a Hogarthian grimace at the social butterfly. She is, oh so radiantly common! Her dress of clamorous iridescence no more contains her impudent, firm flesh than the gold-coloured pupa contains the emergent moth. Cynthia resembles the female of the Purple Emperor in that, in alimentation, she prefers the vitiated. You might describe her in this comedy as a vulgar modern quean going a progress through the guts of publicity. She will end, you feel sure, on the screen. During Marjorie's long first act recital of the events leading up to the divorce court it was Cynthia's face that I watched. It showed a quality of content positively ghoulish. As the play progressed the actress seemed to me to take her colleagues by the tips of her intelligent fingers and drop them one by one into the well of the orchestra. She captured the finer appreciation equally with the grosser laughter. To my great grief, half-way through the play we lost Cynthia. Interest then devolved, or was supposed to devolve, upon Marjorie. Personally, I endured the last act hoping against hope for one more glimpse of Miss Evans. But it was not to be.

There is one matter in which I have a suggestion to make to the management. It is that either they should rid themselves of this too triumphant lady, or print her name on the posters in the tubes and other places in letters at least as large as those assigned to her colleagues. The present practice is not only discourteous; it is nonsensical.

A Spectacle for Spectacles

Decameron Nights, by Boccaccio ? English Version by a
Lot of People. Drury Lane.

DEEMING THE REOPENING OF
Charles the Second's playhouse in Drury
Lane a matter of general interest, and in the
absence of the usual invitation, I made formal
application for a seat at any reasonably early performance. The management regretted that the house was
" sold out for some time to come." One rejoiced, for the
old theatre's sake. Popular paragraphists had written
of all-night vigil at the doors, of Royal patronage, of
tumbling seas of success. Murmuring, " I will drown
and no discourtesy shall save me," I obtained through
one of the agencies a seat in a back row of the Upper
Circle. On Monday, at the fifth performance of
Decameron Nights, I counted thirteen empty boxes and
some thirty or forty vacant seats in my immediate
vicinity. The theatrical agency had offered me choice
of stalls, which I refused. It occurred to me that this
was an occasion upon which to judge from a popular
seat a production for which the house was " sold out."

That same night, intrigued, as they say, by the
calculated assault upon eye and ear and the wilful disregard of the spectator's intellectual and emotional
faculties, I made some jottings for an article which

A Spectacle for Spectacles

would not, however, shape itself. Out of temper, I decided to banish until the morning Boccaccio and Mr. Robert McLaughlin, the Renaissance and Mr. Herman Finck, the forty-five speaking actors and Mr. Arthur Collins himself. I took down a volume of the old periodical, "Vanity Fair," and there came across a criticism of a performance of a "romantic play with music" of fifty years ago. "Feeble but moral plot. Music sprightly. Scenery and effects startling. Singing good and costumes elaborate. No acting." Such blessed positivity, I surmised with a trifle of envy, could have proceeded only from the stalls. It is difficult not to make up your mind about something an inch from your nose. But up there that night it had been different. The popular part of an audience must keep its popular distance. Had these distant ones been amused? I certainly had not. Nor, I gathered, had the decent people about me. They sate glum. In the interval I overheard a fragment of talk between the Upper Circle bar-attendant and a smartly dressed young woman. "How d'you like it, dearie?" asked Hebe. "Showy," replied her lady friend, "Very showy. But isn't it a bit dull?"

It is not my intention to counter managerial discourtesy with vague disparagement. Let me rather consider what means exist for the impassioning of an audience seated at such distance that not only the actor's facial play, but his very identity is lost. I admire intensely the miming of Miss Ellis Jeffreys. I know by heart every shade of her admirable expressiveness. At Drury Lane she presented me with a blank mask. My eyesight is good, yet until the actress

A Spectacle for Spectacles

spoke I did not recognize her. She was a speck on the seashore, seen from some beetling cliff. So all the players. Miss Gladys Ancrum, giving vent to a full-throated lullaby in the shadow of a huge Florentine state-bed, was like Edgar's " tall anchoring bark diminished to her cock." I found myself computing whether twice the singer's height would reach to the tester, of the top of which I had full view, and whether there was room for yet a third Miss Ancrum between the tester and the flies. I ran my eye round the circle and rejoiced to know my seat was higher than these. I was jealous of the gallery. So children dispute about mountain-tops. And all the time these little puppets were having a tragic time of it down there, among themselves, on that far-away beach. Life's shipwreck. But none of us had cared if the waves had swept them all away. I know of hardly any actor who can hold an audience through the reverse end of an opera-glass. Vesta Tilley and Grock certainly, Sir Harry Lauder and Lockhart's Elephants perhaps. But no " legitimate " actor. Sarah, dissolving the stalls in tears, fusses incredibly about nothing, seen from the chandelier. Let me absolve the Drury Lane actors, then, from blame for ineffectiveness. Miss Jeffreys quite rightly made up her mind to be audible, and plastered the Upper Circle wall with intention. She underlined every sentence and every word. I can form no opinion of what her performance was like from the stalls; up there we were grateful for it. An actor, whom I could not recognize, had some fine gestures and looked like a smart young Saladin of the toyshops. An indistinguishable little lady, name of Perdita, prattled in engaging

A Spectacle for Spectacles

American. A tall dark villain leaped about the stage like Remendado pursued by Dancairo's whip. But who these personages were and what like they were it was impossible to say. I remember seeing Tessandier play *L'Arlésienne*, first in a small theatre in Marseilles, where she was overwhelming, and then in the Arena at Arles, where she was quite ineffective. Yet the performance was the same. Acting at 300 feet is perhaps non-existent. The Greeks knew this, wore masks and walked about on stilts. But they did not act in our sense of the word. Rhetoric, too, not dialogue, is needed to span any considerable gulf. Mr. Hewlett or M. Maurice Donnay might reproduce Boccaccio's humour in a small intimate theatre. But joking at Drury Lane is like being witty in a high wind; leap-frog were better. And even verbal leap-frog disappoints when it comes like the strokes of cricketers in a far-away field to the beholder on a mountain top. " What would you do if your husband deceived you ? " somebody asked Miss Jeffreys. Faintly the words floated up. But before we caught their significance the lady had unaccountably squatted herself on the top of a chest containing the deceiver. An appreciable interval, and then the explanatory " Sit on him ! " No. Drama, acting, wit are impossible at the Lane.

Scenery and the dresses remain, and alas! no expense has been spared. Once again indiscriminate lavishness in the theatre has proved its own punishment. " The Royal Hanging Gardens, Damascus," so dazzle the eye that literally nothing can be seen. Exquisite, doubtless, in detail, the scene in bulk affects you like an overgrown shop-window stocked with every

A Spectacle for Spectacles

sort of cushion and lampshade. Not an inch of space is left undecorated, from the henna-stained heels of the dancers to the panache of Saladin himself, whom you can hardly see for myrmidons. Lamb complained, you remember, of that picture of the son of Nun declaiming, " Sun, stand thou still upon Gibeon, and thou, Moon, in the valley of Ajalon," that the eye could not detect which was Joshua. So in Mr. Collins's picture I could not for some time make out which was Saladin. His greater light was made obsequious to the lesser whole. In " The Piazzo di San Marco, Venice," the Doge spoke for full five minutes before I could locate him. The only rests for the eye in these deserts of brightness were provided by some comparatively sombre scarlet cockatoos and the brown legs of the slaves. Musically, the piece went with a cheerful clatter. Mr. Herman Finck preserves the courage of his musical opinions. Now I like Mr. Finck's tunes and often hum them. He is the best of the revue bunch. Whether the Crusaders gave up their swords to music admirably suited to the Pender Troupe of Giants or whether the Lady Teodora would warble one of Miss José Collins's waltz songs, seems to me immaterial. The banality of such tunefulness as this is its popular safeguard. The decorum of the play is unexceptionable. I have seen wilder frenzies among Messrs. Lyons's waitresses than these *coryphées* afford.

Now how about that alternative to disparagement ? Were I Mr. Collins I should not have asked for a better play, better actors, or a better singer than Miss Ancrum. That would not have helped in that house. But I should have saved a small fortune over the

A Spectacle for Spectacles

scenery and dresses, and put some of it into the brains of a producer who was also an artist. I should have sent for M. Stowitz and asked him how, in those few minutes at the New Oxford, he manages to crowd in so much of the spirit of Boccaccio. And I should certainly have sent for a musician, preferably Mr. Norman O'Neill, and asked him for melody and beauty. I should have gone bankrupt, you say. Fortunately, Mr. Collins is immune from that contingency. Is not the house " sold out for some time to come " ?

Maids, your Toast!

Blood and Sand, by Vincente Blasco Ibañez. Adapted by Tom Cushing. New Theatre.

RAVELLING LAST SUMMER FROM Shrewsbury to London I whiled away the journey in contemplation of a country maid. Obviously of the domestic class, " strong, not afraid of work," she had the " Shropshire look " so highly commended in registry offices. Heedless of stretched vistas of servitude, " nine in family, two kept, one evening a week, no followers," the poor lamb pastured her soul on present romance. In her hand of raw pink she clutched, and with her faithful eyes devoured, a novelette: " Manuel, or the Bull-fighter of Madrid." I did not think of my little maid until the performance of *Blood and Sand*. And then I saw her, distinctly, in the front row of the Upper Circle. She held some soldier's hand, but I felt that her mind was not upon prosaic him, but upon wonderful Mr. Matheson Lang and fabulous Miss Lillah McCarthy. Not yet, I saw in her startled countenance after the scene of upbraiding and recrimination, not yet had it been her lot to dust chairs and tables magnificent as those at the feet of which, cast down by her re-generate lover, lay prone a " vampire " in the flesh. One felt that this scene embodied the waking ecstasies

Maids, your Toast!

of half the areas of London, and one vowed, for a sennight, to ring upon no bell.

Whenever I think of the power of transmutation possessed by simple hearts I am filled with envy. It is good to be able to gild preposterous things, to turn the pretentious to glamour. For me romance is a native bird, easily flushed in home stubble, less easily in foreign furrows. I am never farther from its spirit than when I listen to these exotic plays in which the romantic is treated as something extrinsic, foreign to everyday knowledge. I found Mr. Lang's matador an unusual, but not a romantic figure. He was a joy to the eye, and the actor reproduced with infinite skill the flamboyances of the *rasta*. But I was no more in his skin than in that of Cetewayo or Umslopogaas. He was romantic only in the sense that the anthropophagi are romantic. I learned nothing of his mind and desired to learn nothing. Now I happen to have known, intimately, a retired bull-fighter. He was, at the time of our acquaintance, a checker on a hay-press in the South of France. He was extraordinarily unlike Mr. Matheson Lang. Slight in figure, and wistful, almost dejected in mind, you would have said a druggist unable to meet his liabilities. Yet, with his past glories and present miseries, he seemed to me exquisitely romantic. I knew the heart of him, yet he remained inscrutable. Romance is entirely a matter of mental outlook. The outlook of this play's bull-fighter is that of one of his bulls. The outlook of his enchantress is that of a creature of the films. Three hours of the two are less romantic than five minutes of Kipps and Anne Pornick. I do not know exactly what words I

Maids, your Toast!

expect to hear when a Doña Sol sets about inveigling
an El Gallardo. But remembering my Spaniards of the
hay-press I want to hear, at least from the man of
peasant origin, common Spanish speech interpreted and
made real. I want tang and bite which I can translate
into actuality. What I heard was the commonplaces of
Hyde Park on Sunday afternoon. " Am I nice ? "
asked the lady, arch as any nursemaid. " You are very
tempting," replied the bull-fighter. The tones were the
soul-stirring ones of Mr. Lang, but the sentiment was
that of the guardsman's " Not 'arf! " " Git away
closer! " came the giggling rebuke. This, I admit, is
pure nursemaid. Miss McCarthy did not giggle. Her
" Go away; sit over there! " was uttered with the
utmost stateliness. Miss McCarthy was, in point of
fact, too stately. She poured out a drink for her
" superb animal " with all the unction of an officiating
priestess. Aware that foreign houris gesticulate, she
gesticulated handsomely, but the gestures did not
spring from her words. Loveliness this actress possesses, but in this part it was the loveliness of the shell
left by the tide. She expressed beauty without meaning,
recalled the blameless partner of Mr. Wilson Barrett's
woolly raptures. You remember how Marcus and
Mercia, with the lions roaring up-stage, kept a steadfast
face to their admirers. Even if the beasts had got loose,
you felt that the actors would have maintained their
front. So when the matador, intent on murder, came
crashing through the window behind her, did Doña Sol
firmly resist any impulse to look round. Perhaps the
grande amoureuse of Spain is unreal; perhaps Mr.
Ibañez has not created a real figure; perhaps Mr. Tom

Maids, your Toast!

Cushing is not a very skilful adapter. I can only contrast Miss McCarthy's performance with that of Réjane in a similar rôle in Abel Hermant's *Trains de Luxe*. There were vice and passion unbridled; in the voice of the great actress the neigh and whimper of the horse, in her nostrils luxury, in her gait riot. Miss McCarthy, though extravagant in manner, betrayed no real passion or appetite, laid bare not any soul, but only her back. I am getting tired of these implications of the costumier, and can never behold these undraped expanses without recalling Villiers de l'Isle-Adam's condemnation of the night-sky as a waste of advertising space. When Mr. Lang emerged from his scene of passion his coat was white as a miller's. But my housemaid is a faithful little soul; she did not even titter. Perhaps the utmost of her reflection was that master's clothes would need an extra good brush in the morning. I urge Miss McCarthy to put more clothes on Doña Sol's back and give her something better than a film-mentality. Réjane's dresses fastened at the throat; her genius laid her smallest impulse bare.

The plot of the play is really very quaint. El Gallardo is so unnerved by his intrigue that when next he appears in the arena he breaks his leg. This mended, he threatens his faithless paramour with a revolver, reads her a sermon on which our own Bishop Welldon could not improve, and finally lays her flat both in spirit and in body. A tower of morality, he rushes off to fight another bull. But virtue turns out to be a frail prop, since he breaks his leg again. Perhaps this does not matter very much, his wife having exacted, in true wifeliness, the sacrifice of his career as the price of her for-

Maids, your Toast!

giveness. How, I wonder, would it be if playwrights were to clear their minds of cant and realize that it is stupid to turn a story of a matador and his light-o'-love into a morality for the servants' hall ? How if they were to realize that to a popular hero of the standing of a professional boxer or footballer, a doxy more or less is of no great moment ? *Carmen*, I would point out to them, is not concerned with morality until the last few bars. Nor is morality in any way concerned with the present play. There is probably a Spanish version of the French philosophy: *Je te plais. Tu me plais. Aimons-nous!* I have little doubt that an El Gallardo would, in real life, have stabbed the woman, which would have made a stirring melodrama. What, knowing something of Spaniards, I say with confidence, is that he would not have lectured her. If our playwrights must wind up their plays with a moral, let them at least leave Spain and the bull-ring out of it. Do our bowling-greens lack champions ? I will wager, however, that there are enough serving-maids in London to fill the New Theatre for a year. And since I heard one person, whom I judged to have the mind, but not the status, of a housemaid, declare the play to be the " sweetest ever," I do not doubt that it will draw adherents from above-stairs.

West of Suez

East of Suez, by Somerset Maugham. His Majesty's
Theatre.

IPPING, ONE DAY, INTO THE SIX-
penny box of a second-hand bookseller, I
came across an old account of the London
stage. Therein I read the sad story of
Nitocris, the great Egyptian spectacle-drama; how the
Nile was turned into a grotto to drown a bunch of con-
spirators, but without arousing enthusiasm; how all the
gods of Egypt were carried in procession, but to no
popular purpose. Drury Lane had hissed and in the
" Examiner " next morning Henry Morley advised the
author to turn the thing into a pantomime and get rid
of the words. I was to visit His Majesty's that evening,
and I trembled. Would Mr. Dean avoid the old
mistake of drowning the play in excess of spectacle ?
True that he had spoken of restoring this theatre to a
state of lesser absurdity; yet those hordes of real Chinamen threatened disquietingly.

My apprehensions were ill-founded. In *East of Suez*
it was the play which swamped the spectacle. " The
man recovered of the bite, the dog it was that died."
The beginning was most promising. The overture, for
which the lights were scrupulously lowered, turned out
to be a most ingenious piece of musical leg-pulling.
Mr. Goossens had made no pretence of absorbing China

as Mackenzie did the British Empire and Sibelius Finland, and then giving his emotions back in terms of his own art. He had simply reproduced the cat-calls of the East on Western stops and strings, and left the task of regurgitation to the audience. To Western ears this is not music, although to the Celestials it may make an exquisite tone poem. One needed, to hear sympathetically, a Chinese dressing-gown, or at some Promenade Concert under Peking skies to watch the chopstick of a Hen Ri Wu. There are, however, always a number of people who, the less they understand, the more they are impressed. (See any German shopkeeper confronted with Goethe's *Faust*.) The simple, musically speaking, among the audience at His Majesty's doubtless took this cleverly executed little joke of Mr. Goossens for the sublimer recondities, and disposed themselves to mystery. The curtain rises upon a scene of babel of which no word reaches our comprehension. Orientals, adorned with the bowler of European culture and chattering from the teeth outwards, proffer their extortionate bargains in cheap watches, picture postcards, the meaningless frippery of the Occident. They look as secret and as wise as monkeys. From time to time a white man is thrown up on this yellow flood, concealing by the grave carriage of his body the natural defects of his European mind. The shopkeepers put up their shutters. One of them, belated, is mildly admonished by the native policeman. A British sailor yields to a street-walker. " Good-bye " the native policeman calls after them from the shadow of the gateway. It is night. I do not know if this is like China; but I do know that it is extraordinarily like the old port

West of Suez

at Marseilles. At this point, alas! we took leave of Mr. Dean. His frontispiece pointed to a tale of Loti; the drama was to ſtray no farther than Streatham.

And now I am in a difficulty. Mr. Somerset Maugham is a writer of great diſtinction, yet he has written a quite insincere play. I am convinced that Mr. Maugham knows China or knows, at leaſt, that China is not Europe. I feel he realizes very definitely that the root of the trouble between English men and Eurasian women is the English code of morals. But his play shows that he diſtruſts his medium, that he is aware he muſt not say openly that what is the matter with these mixed unions is their legality. He does say it, ultimately, but then only by implication. In the meantime there are three hours to be filled in after a fashion which shall be acceptable to Streatham. This, of course, spells sentimentality, in which Mr. Maugham is not in the leaſt interested; and this, I think, explains why *Eaſt of Suez* rings so exceedingly untrue. If you may not speak truth one artificiality is as good as another. To the artiſt there is little discriminating in insincerities, and Mr. Maugham, who can be an extraordinarily fine and faſtidious artiſt when he likes, has here turned on the oldeſt of conventions. The two commonplace Englishmen in this play, each morally worth, to us who believe in their code, the whole jabbering crew of the firſt scene, are yet dramatically less intereſting. Those others elude us, we know what these will do. One upright fellow will insiſt upon marriage with the Eurasian woman who, unknown to him, has been the miſtress of a Chinaman and has also been engaged to his beſt friend. That other upright fellow will, after a

214

thousand protestations, court the lady again, and shoot himself upon discovery. There is a model for plays about women who, for any reason, are *déclassées*, and Mr. Maugham has used it. "You may dive into many waters, but there is *one* social Dead Sea——!" is what, in effect, the new Cayley Drummle says to the friend who is about to announce his forthcoming marriage. And later, "I should like to express my regret, Aubrey, for the way in which I spoke of George Orreyed's marriage." Only the names are altered. At its vital point Mr. Maugham, like Pinero, burks the issue. Paula's ruin springs not from the fact that she is a courtesan at heart, but from a coincidence; Daisy is defeated not because she is a Eurasian, but because she is Daisy. Yet both plays set out to prove that if the class is "not nice" you cannot afford to have anything to do with it. Touch pitch and you will be defiled. Both plays prove a particular case from which we are to deduce an unwarrantable conclusion. But Streatham doesn't want to know about a particular Daisy; it wants to hear that all marriages with Eurasians are fatal, and so keep its menfolk. Above all, it wants to shut its eyes to the way in which they may be kept. That at which Mr. Maugham hints, and would say if he dare, is that the passion of both men is not unreasonable, but anti-social, not unlawful, but inexpedient. Very few things are immoral which are sincere, and the real point of view of European ladies is not that they object to the inevitable, which is silly, but to the recognition of it entailed by marriage. The mistresses of their menfolk can be ignored; wives must be called upon. We feel that if Daisy had been mistress instead of wife, the lover would

215

not have betrayed his friend, so strange is the European code. The betrayer shoots himself, not because of his sin against morality, but in deference to the *convenances*. He blushes to do openly that of which he is not, at heart, ashamed. He fears social ostracism. Daisy's passion is to entwine her arms about her lover and with him to sit upon a hill-side watching the rice grow, " for ever," as the poet puts it, " in a deep deliberate bliss, a spirit sliding through tranquillity." That tranquillity is to be induced, she carefully explains, by opium. Whereupon the pistol-shot. What Mr. Maugham is careful not to explain is that the lover was quite willing to sit on the hill-side for such time as he could do so under the cover of adultery. It is a curious situation. Streatham hopes that by doing away with these marriages these unaccountable hankerings will come to an end. Mr. Maugham knows that strange desire will persist, but that if there is to be no bother there must be no marriage. He knows that between such outspokenness and the British stage are arrayed all the forces of law and order, the censorship and public opinion, army, navy, and the police. He knows that his play is to be performed at His Majesty's before an audience as to whose intelligence he has no illusions. And so he fills in those three hours with perfunctory heart-searchings after the manner of Sir Arthur Pinero in the days which were before Paula. The proper title of this play is *Daisy's Escapade*. And all the time that fascinating crowd from the docks, about whom Mr. Maugham could tell us so much, is idle. I do not blame the author, but the theatre to which he conforms.

The play was perfectly acted by our friends, who had

West of Suez

no European conventions to contend against, and fairly well by the English actors within those conventions. But I should have dearly liked to know what the impassive Oriental thought of the hysterical Englishman whose mouth is as full of " love " as a dressmaker's is of pins.

The Way of a Goose

The Way of an Eagle, by Ethel M. Dell. Adelphi Theatre.

ORGIVE, FOR ITS APPOSITENESS, A reminiscence. The place was the pebbled wilderness of the Crau, that unnatural desert of mid-Provence ringed about with natural growth like a priest's tonsure, the time hot noon on a day in late July. The car in which I must potter about unheroic hayfields had broken down, and "the maist o' four hours" was all the prediction which a mechanical Scot would vouchsafe to one unversed in ironmongery. In all the baked landscape no sign of life beyond a pair of brown puttees wriggling in the yellow dust; no sound save the monotonous cri-cri of the cicada in the thyme. *Lou soulèu me fai canta.* Yes, indeed! Both sun and insect were pitiless. Oh to be a Buddhist, inured to the sun and possessive of one's bored soul! I searched my pockets for a scrap of print and found none. And then, among the jacks and spanners under the driver's up-ended seat, I espied a tattered paper-back by an author whom, unperused, I had yet despised. In this book an unrightful lord escorts a high-born lady round the acres of his usurpation. The ponies in the phaeton take fright, as also does his lordship, who incontinently jumps. Jumps, too, a velveteen Adonis, in guise of an under-gardener. Dropping spud and hoe he, like a circus-

The Way of a Goose

rider, measures his arc, strikes chord from flower-bed to park drive, leaps box, and pulls the pair upon their haunches within stride of level-crossing and signalled express. This much I note, that though the author has a poor eye for humanity he has a good one for horseflesh. The car is mended with twenty anxious pages yet to go. "He gets the lassie," volunteers my dour friend, revealing a human heart. "And he's an earl in his ain richt!" The journey home is beguiled with talk of books, this A.S.C. driver and I confessing a common taste. So may a touch of Garvice make the whole world kin.

Not even the most popular playwright is to be condemned unseen. Hopefully I submitted myself to Miss Dell's latest essay. Perhaps none of the palpitating fair at the Adelphi Theatre doubted the ultimate ability of Nick Ratcliffe, that eagle in his own right, to capture the fluttersome lassie in the end. Probably none but myself was unversed in Dellacruscan procrastinations. Was I right in thinking the eagle's swoops a shade too magnifical? Would not lesser tactics have prevailed? It is a common failing to be a dab hand at big things and a poor one at little. It is probable that Burke was not much of an after-dinner speaker, and that your European strategist would fail at the detail for forming fours. Forgive a story. There was once a lion-hunter who missed his aim. The beast, springing, jumped too far and overleaped his man. Returning next day to the same spot the hunter espied the lion engaged upon some curious evolutions. He was practising short jumps!

But first my readers must learn something of the plot. Muriel Roscoe, having accompanied her father on one

The Way of a Goose

of those punitive expeditions in which the natives do the punishing, is handed over by him to the care of a dare-devil subordinate. The Colonel is killed. Nick disguises himself as an Arab and, wrapping a *burnous* round every part of Muriel—whom he has previously doped—but forgetting to conceal her white high-heeled boots, bears her through the attacking hordes. These naturally take the lady for one of their dead. Now was there ever such a goose as Muriel ? Saved by Nick from a wandering knife, she emits those frantic cacklings proper to stage-geese baulked of an unpleasant end. "I hate you!" she shrieks, stamping that high white heel. But Nick is not swayed. These words of hers move him as much as those of the Poor Man moved Gaveston.

"As if a goose would play the porcupine,
And dart her plumes, thinking to pierce my breast."

Soon afterwards Muriel engages herself to Nick. But the news leaking out that she had spent the night an inanimate bundle on her lover's shoulder, our heroine is of opinion that anserine chastity demands flight. The eagle here performs prodigies of verbal swooping, but with none effect. To paraphrase " Hudibras ":

"A goose convinced against her will
Will hold the same opinion still."

J'ever see such a fowl ? as Henley might have said. Returned to England, Muriel now engages herself to a V.C. with some habit of innocent philandering. In the conduct of his intrigue with a married woman the writer is " niceness " itself. The eagle again makes rhetorical

descent. The V.C. shall elope with the married woman
—not so nice, this—whilst he to his eyrie, to dive no
more save at his victim's bidding. An irrelevant shipwreck sweeps away the V.C.—irrelevant except that in
the perception that an amorist may possess physical
courage we get a redemptive piece of horse-sense. Mr.
Garvice's plea in extenuation was purely equine, Miss
Dell's is at least human. Once more the eagle hovers,
dropping to save Muriel's life. Or does she save his?
One is not sure. A few dabs and pecks of commonplace speech, showing unmistakable signs of practice
in short swoops, and the goose is won.

Now I am to declare that there is more risk in sheer
silliness—Miss Dell's play is far more silly than Mr.
Garvice's novel—than the people who dabble in it
realize. To play with the passions and not know that
they are fire is peculiarly dangerous. I imagine that
considerably less harm would have been done to the
Adelphi audience by a performance of, say, the censored
Mrs. Warren's Profession. Admitted that Mr. Shaw's
play might have revealed an unpleasant minor truth,
Miss Dell's uncensored nonsense contracts all life to a
single imperfectly comprehended obsession. It shows
man enamoured of the Imbecile. The playwright here
follows an old model. It was "the softness of mind,
amounting almost to feebleness which rendered Lucy
even dearer" to the manly Edgar Ravenswood. In
Miss Dell's play the composition is balanced by depicting the woman as being in a state of primitive sensual
savagery, in which the violence of the male is the
female's most cherished pride. Again the authoress is
not the first in the field. An Austrian novelist, one

The Way of a Goose

Leopold von Sacher-Masoch, has depicted the pleasure taken by certain abnormal types in abuse and cruelty inflicted by their lovers. Our present heroine is a victim of subconscious aberration. Now there can be no intellectual objection to such a study presented in proper perspective before a discriminatory audience by a psychiatrist who knows his material. There is every objection to amateur exposition in front of a middle-class audience. Savagery, sensual or otherwise, may not do much harm to the savage. The submission of the drab to her bully—one of the commonest variants of the formula in this play—has a sentimental tinge which analysis may not show to be debasing. Before mentality can be debased it must exist. But the audience at the Adelphi was entirely respectable. These good people had an undoubted mentality, inclined though it might be to the mawkish; and I cannot see that anything but harm could be done to that mentality by asking it to accept an undeniable Masochist as a normal type.

Perhaps it is a mistake to gird too whole-heartedly at the Censorship. That musty institution may need remodelling only. The licence of an alleged "improper" play should be endorsed: "The subject-matter of this piece renders it fit for performance before educated audiences only." *The Way of an Eagle* should be returned marked "Perfectly proper material. The silliness of treatment amounting to impropriety, licence is refused."

Iago's Ancestress

The Medea, by Euripides. Translated by Gilbert Murray. New Theatre.

S I LISTENED, AT THE NEW Theatre, to Miss Thorndike giving tongue to Medea, and watched how admirably she held that fury in leash, my mind went back to a confession once made in the "Saturday Review" by Mr. Max Beerbohm. A confession of boredom, occasioned by a performance, at the Court Theatre, of the *Eleĉtra*. The ſtage had been darkened, it appeared, to a groping twilight ill-suited to the clear-cut Greek thought, and the aĉtors had spoken too slowly. Then followed a sentence which so shocked my youthful reverence— Greek drama howsoever produced was not, in Mancheſter, to be spoken of lightly—that it has ſtuck in my mind to this day. " A Greek tragedy in a modern theatre, however perfeĉtly it be enaĉted, is bound to be tedious." Soon afterwards, at the Trocadero in Paris, I saw Racine's *Andromaque*—which for the nonce I muſt pretend is a Greek play—quite perfeĉtly done by Bartet and Paul Mounet, who reeled the thing off at high speed and in the glare of high noon. Yet never have I been so bored in any theatre, except during those parts of *Phèdre* when Sarah has not been on the ſtage. The famous *récit de Théramène*, that synonym for dullness, seems to me to apply to all dramas about Greeks; any

223

Iago's Ancestress

simulated or even genuine taste for which reminds me of our neighbour's aphorism concerning married love: *C'est bizarre, mais ce n'est pas défendu.*

I was not bored on Monday afternoon. On the contrary I found the greatest possible interest in watching three great artists in reticence and implication tackle this huge outspoken drama, the personages of which must fling their voices against a sky of sullen brass, hallooing their hates to the reverberate hills. Players of greater fame, whose art I had not known so intimately, would have delighted me in this play hardly at all. Setting aside the exquisiteness of Professor Murray's translation, beneath which the athletic Greek verse stirs like Jason's muscles under the silken skin, let me consider a little closely this study of a woman transformed by injury into a living Curse. "Her wrongs and her hate fill all the sky." Now I am not certain that hate, unqualified and unennobled, is worth anybody's while. It wasn't worth Herr Lissauer's pettifogging while, and I am not sure that it does not degrade Euripides. His thesis would seem to be that cruelty is doubly vile, not only because it causes pain to the victim, but because it makes a worse man of him. Professor Murray deplores that this grim lesson, taught too often by history, is too seldom preached by the poets. Frankly, I am not quite sure that this is a doctrine which ought to be preached, or how far it is consonant with the old theorem of purgation by pity and awe. The only pity in the *Medea* is expressed by the Chorus, a boring lot of young women feebly enlarging upon what has gone before like a poor parson marring a good text. And the awe, surely, was to proceed from the fear aroused in the

Iago's Ancestress

breast of the spectator that through moral weakness he might meet a similar fate. Now I, the spectator to be awed, conceive easily that I might be such a fool as Jason, but not that at the vilest I could, being sane, become Medea. I have neither belief nor interest in people whose hate fills all the sky. I hardly credit Iago's comparatively puny distemper. He, one must think, was insane; and it is to be noted that Shakespeare relegates him to the plane of secondary interest. Medea, too, was insane. No sane woman slaughters her babes to spite her man, any more than her man will, literally, cut off his nose to spite his face. That the insanity of Medea is bigger than life-size is simply an aggravation. One really cannot, or at least I cannot, find tragic interest in monstrosity. Strip the *Medea* of its poetic clothing, and only the monstrous remains. Strip any big play of Shakespeare of its music, and the bones are those of humanity. It is possible that, on the Greek stage, where the male actors wore stilts and were so muffled as to be unrecognizable as human beings, the non-humanity of a play's characters did not matter. Played by a breathing woman, the non-humanity of Medea irritates at least one modern spectator intensely; it irritates me to see exquisite speech and magnificently ordered action hung upon characters which are unreal. And when, at the end, Zeus puts his finger in the pie to protect from human vengeance the pitiless woman who has schemed so elaborately to save her own skin, why then I lose all semblance of interest. The intervention of the god resembles the patent-medicine advertisement which, at the foot of a column, is guaranteed to assuage the excruciating agonies entrancingly set forth above.   And, in this case, it is a lying advertisement.

> " To you, lord governor,
> Remains the censure of this hellish villain,
> The time, the place, the torture; O, enforce it! "

is the poet's remedy for Iago.   " The end men looked for cometh not " is no cure.   Medea, we feel, deserved more than she got.   That cruelty turned her into a vile thing is not the fault of cruelty, but of the degenerative metal upon which it was exercised.   Medea was not essentially noble, but base; she would fit, as a spitfire, into any Shavian comedy.   That she should go gadding about Pallas' plain in a golden chariot is, to an English mind, scarcely a fitting reward.   What propriety there was here to the Greek mind I can but guess; watching the play in the English theatre of to-day, I care nothing for such fiddle-faddle.   We have outgrown these too big emotions.   Opera is their sphere, with Strauss to make divine hash of them.

Miss Thorndike bent up every corporal, mental, and spiritual agent to fill out her tremendous part.   Moreover—and this was indeed a triumph—she did not once bring her nerves into play, delivering herself of tragic matter as such stuff ought to be delivered.   Medea has few moments of tenderness; one, with the children, was most admirably found.   I think that another actress, say Sarah, might perhaps have seized one opportunity which Miss Thorndike missed.   It occurred at the lines:

> " And she who, labouring long, shall find some way
> Whereby her lord may bear with her, nor fray

226

Iago's Ancestress

His yoke too fiercely, blessed is the breath
That woman draws! Else let her pray for death."

I can imagine the exquisite tenderness with which
Sarah would have sighed out that " blessed is the
breath that woman draws." Medea, on Monday, gave
us here the irksome dolour of Jane Clegg. But I can
imagine, too, that in one aspect Miss Thorndike's
performance was unbeatable—that of hardness and
astringency. Sarah would have wanted to charm you *in
spite of* Medea, to show the pathetic victim beneath
the poisoner. This quality of ineffability was in
her Phèdre, and she forced it, willy-nilly, into her
Lucrezia Borgia. She would have got glamour into
Medea, whereas Miss Thorndike realizes simply that
glamour isn't there. Whether, if glamour were there,
the English actress would be able to encompass it is
not the point. Let us give credit where credit is due.
I know no other actress who could have conveyed so
adequately the sense of moral catastrophe, of a mind
thrown down into baseness. Mr. Faber's Jason was
nobly conceived, if a trifle veiled in utterance. The
actor embellished his hero with a most fascinating little
golden beard, composed of separate spirals which, as
he walked, seemed to tinkle like miniature belfries.
Mr. Casson's delivery of the Messenger's speech was a
magnificent piece of declamation, and the Chorus
acquitted itself intelligently and gracefully. The pace
throughout was admirable, the lighting good, and Miss
Thorndike's russet mantle stood out from the autumn-
tinted walls with something of the joy and colour so
plentifully lacking in poor Medea. No, not poor;
nasty, horrid Medea.

227

Metaphysics and Melodrama

The Balance, by Frank Dix and Leon M. Lion. Strand Theatre.

HE TRIAL SCENE IN *THE BALANCE*, at the Strand Theatre, at the close of which an innocent man is condemned to death, is an offence against dramatic propriety and good manners. This is the greater pity in that the earlier acts of this melodrama by Messrs. Frank Dix and Leon M. Lion contain much which, after its kind, is interesting and likeable. The scene at the Old Bailey, dreadful in the strict sense, is an irrelevant horror of purely morbid appeal, presenting just that view of a murder trial which delights the vulture's eye of Sunday's carrion-journalist: the fainting spectator, the filing out of the jury, the suspense, the calling of the jurymen's names, the awful apostrophe of the Judge. We are invited to gape at the trappings of death, to listen, for the fun of the thing, to the most appalling of all pronouncements. The actor who impersonated the Judge forgot his words on the first night and had to be prompted. This incident, trivial in any other circumstance, brought one sharply to the perception that this was mummery, and mummery not in any way to be justified. I felt a guilty creature to be sitting at such a play.

There isn't, really, any aesthetic justification for sheer horror. It is a whip to jaded appetite, it provides good

Metaphysics and Melodrama

scope for acting, and it accords with a recognized kink in human nature. (One enjoys many things which it would be difficult to justify; Chinamen, we know, will sit for hours watching simulated scenes of torture, though it may be doubted whether this is enjoined upon them by Confucius.) Further, one comes to regard the characters in a Grand Guignol play simply as models for experiment, as " cases " pure and simple, with which we take care not to establish human relationship. If our authors had presented their Old Bailey scene as a separate " turn," we had not, perhaps, minded so much. They present it, however, as the pendant to a scene of admirable actuality, not as a consequence of a crime, but as a mere fluke of miscarrying justice. The murder is an act of vengeance upon a scoundrel who, after brow-beating and goading a poor wretch, finally debauches his wife. The last act would have had the Galsworthian sanctions if the dock had held not the innocent but the guilty. That a human being with whom we have every human sympathy should come to be hanged is a dreadful thing, but one which, since it happens, may be shown. The justification for the portrayal of a dreadful thing must be two-fold. It must be dramatically proper, whereby we mean inevitable; it must be proper on the score of manners. This is achieved when we are reminded that every man should be prepared to witness and even to do that which he reasonably deputes the law to do for him. It may be argued that since innocent men are sometimes condemned to death, that, too, may be portrayed. Not so. In the depicting of accident there is no aesthetic propriety.

Metaphysics and Melodrama

Or our authors may say that their play is a melodrama, and not a tragedy. Leaving out the question of musical accompaniment, and also that definition of tragedy which would make of it a conflict between two ideas of right, I cannot see any essential difference between the two. The difference is superficial, surely, one of treatment rather than of subject. Melodrama, says my dictionary, is " a drama abounding in romantic sentiment and agonizing situations "—a definition which, ignoring what the pedants may have to say about the word " romantic," I am perfectly prepared to apply to the tragedy of *King Lear*. Perhaps we may say that tragedy is the matter of melodrama ennobled by poetry, whereas melodrama is the stuff of tragedy degraded by triviality. Tragedy teaches the spectator that if he be as big a fool as the hero he will come by the same nasty end. It " learns " him to be a fool. The highbrow view of melodrama seems to be that since its misfortunes happen to none but fools, serious interest is uncalled for. That way, surely, disillusion lies. If the spectator is to enjoy farce, the actors must take it seriously; if he is to enjoy melodrama, then he himself must take it seriously. The gallery at the Strand Theatre showed an inclination to huzza, and the stalls to titter, when the heroine declared her intention of selling her body that the fruits of her shame might provide fruit for the invalid. Now it seems to me that, according to their lights, the gallery had the clearer vision. Should she, or should she not, they inwardly debated; and put it to the cheer. The young woman was to me a thousand times more sympathetic than tragedy's pale prig, Isabella. The father, rounding on his wayward daughter

230

Metaphysics and Melodrama

with the epithet which old Fleming hurled at Dahlia, is real with a dash of irony which the gallery appreciates. The old rogue does not really care, but in the presence of the quality it is fitting that he should make pretence of caring. He is one of those moralists of whom the popular ballad says quaintly, and with finality:

" In a quiet country village
    Her aged parents live;
They drink the champagne wot she sends them,
    But they never can forgive."

The gallery knows this verse, and if the stalls don't know it they ought to. The boxes may object that they are distressed by melodrama's medium of expression; the gallery might say the same of Shakespeare. The root of the matter is in both forms of art, and in the simpler case the gallery seems to me to be the cleverer at divining it. The cleverer because, having the simpler mind, it yet knows how to put that simplicity to its proper use. Heedless of any babble about art, it translates all that is going on down there on the stage into terms of its own experience. We who sit in the stalls should know how to translate in our turn, stop our ears to the commonplace chatter of the commonplace playwright, and reclothe the bones of his play with thought of our own. Somewhere, at some time, some woman has sold her honour, and the fact that a particular dramatist has not thought very nobly thereon does not exempt your intellectuals from doing subtly that which the simple do naturally. Given the proper attitude of surrender to the medium, it is your finest mind who should get the most of enjoyment out of melodrama.

231

Metaphysics and Melodrama

Surrender to emotion, however, is the last thing your theatrical producer demands. Rather will he insist upon surrender to his chairs and tables! I read that Mr. Tom Walls has entrusted the carving of the seats in the Old Bailey scene to the actual carpenter who constructed the original furniture. I can conceive no more dismal revelation of wrong-headedness. Why stop at the actual carpenter? Why not the actual dock itself? " Furniture and Effects in the Trial Scene by the Central Criminal Court. Black Cap kindly lent by Mr. Justice Blank." Faugh! It is because the last act of this play is hung on to scenes which only need sympathetic translation to seem real even to fine minds that I object to it. To condone it because it is " only melodrama " were very villainous criticism. The one gleam of satisfaction in this drab and horrible business is that it does not even come off. We *know* that the proceedings are all a farce, that we are being harrowed to no purpose, that the guilty man will make confession at the end. And therefore we resent the whole business. Mr. George Bealby guyed his part by overplaying, with the exception of an admirable bit at the end. Mr. George Elton was most pathetic, Mr. Sebastian Smith clever, and there was a character sketch of a low-class tout by Mr. Edward Rigby which was so lifelike as almost to take my breath away.

Flights that Failed

The Broken Wing, by Paul Dickey and Charles W.
Goddard. Duke of York's Theatre.
Mr. Budd of Kennington, S.E., by H. F. Maltby.
Royalty Theatre.

OW, I WONDER, DOES IT COME
about that of two extravaganzas—*The Broken
Wing* at the Duke of York's Theatre, and
Mr. Budd of Kennington, S.E., at the Royalty
—I should enjoy one immensely and the other hardly
at all ? Why should silly little Mr. Budd be meat and
drink to me, and those clownish Mexicans no food at
all ? Can it be because, calling Mr. Budd " silly," I am
using the word more carefully than I know ? For
" silly," like so many other beautiful words, has tumbled
downstairs—from blessed innocence to merewitlessness.
Still, on occasion, this luckless vocable keeps about it
some remnant of its fallen day, so that who says " silly
little Mr. Budd," places him lower than the angels,
but on the same landing.

Whereas " clownish," ever a " low " word, has
declined hardly at all, or not more than from the boor
to him who plays it wilfully. And it is under just this
cloak of wilfulness that the hocus-pocus of the theatre
creeps in, and with it that clowning which actors use
when they must simulate something other than

233

Flights that Failed

humanity. With the exception of two, who made display of beauty, the actors in *The Broken Wing*, a "colourful comedy" by Messrs. Paul Dickey and Charles W. Goddard, clowned it to the top of their bent and far beyond any possible lenience of mine. This may not have been the actors' fault; possibly they interpreted their authors exactly. Let me own here to a craving for the portrayal of human beings in the theatre, and none other. This is with me a passion so single that it looks askance at the least show of deceit. I boggle at the Ghost in *Hamlet* and care nothing for that old charlatan, Prospero. Trinculo is my brother, not Ariel; Bully Bottom my familiar, not Puck. Yet in so far as these others are the echo of a human spirit I can get on terms with them. The most attenuated thread of relationship will do. Grock's criticism of life, albeit something metaphysical, is of the purest humanity. I can cope with Ally Sloper, the Mad Hatter, the incarnations of Mr. Billy Merson. I am at home with the lay-figure, that much-libelled mould which common experience has used as its stockpot. I can make something of the topsy-turvy and the distorted, of whatsoever is obedient to or thwartive of Nature. That of which I can make neither head nor tail are those curious stage-creatures made out of a substance which is not in Nature. Ants, said the author of "Religio Medici," are more remarkable than whales or elephants, dromedaries or camels. "In these narrow engines there is more curious mathematics, and the civility of these little citizens more neatly sets forth the wisdom of their Maker."

I have less respect for the greater part of the characters in *The Broken Wing* than I have for the camel or,

Flights that Failed

a fortiori, the ant. Their mathematical system eludes me; I cannot add them up. They seem to me to be uncivil citizens flouting their Maker, " imperfect creatures such as were not preserved in the Ark," but also having neither " seeds nor principles in the womb of Nature." Take that English sea-captain who has lost his ship and now goes maundering about his *patio*, chattering yet communicating nothing. Or that Captain Innocencio dos Santos, a potential Nostromo reduced to the antics of Dancairo in the opera of *Carmen* and killing his superior officer *pour rire*. In this inconsequential country even murder, it would seem, is without consequences. Take Inez, that far from " silly virgin "—Spenser's phrase—who strove not her English lover to with$\mathit{st}$and, but to bring on. Time and again I have been delighted in the music-hall by Miss Maidie Scott's ironic presentation of maidens not too markedly loth. In the legitimate theatre a less frivolous sage has harangued us to the same purpose. " If God makes me fall in love with another woman's husband, that's His look-out," occurring in the Notebooks of Samuel Butler or in a play of his disciple might conceivably cover immensities of implication. Hurled at us as a comic joke, and spoken with the aplomb of an Ethel Levy but without that artist's *diablerie*, the line seems to me to be merely offensive. Inez, in this play, is Bret Harte's Mliss without the tang of sincerity, Saint-Pierre's Virginie without the innocence. An actress of infantile charm might have made an idyllic figure of her; Miss Dorothy Dix, alert and spry, turned her into a hoyden of the Edgware Road. This was the more hurtful inasmuch as the

235

Flights that Failed

object of these unbashful solicitations was exquisitely played. I was offended by the assault as when violence is offered to some beautiful thing. When Mr. Francis Lister, the aviator whose plane has crashed, came upon this stageful of exuberant Mexicans, it was as though a noisy supper-band had fallen back, out of sheer exhaustion, upon some web of dreams. The performance of this actor reminded me throughout of an exquisite moment of James Welch. It was in some play of the circus in which the little fellow had been struck by the ring-master's whip, and his pained " You've hurt me! " opened an abyss of degradation before our eyes. We were ashamed for the bully. So this wounded airman made me ashamed of the sentimental assault upon him, to me horrific beyond words. Mr. Lister's Ferdinand filled the eye; in this present boisterousness he filled the mind with implications of a rarer world. Curiously enough, there was one moment in this garish play in which the scene took on beauty—a simple back-cloth showing sunset over the plain, and against it an idle fellow crooning a song of his people. I have never been to Mexico, and know no larger desert than that pebbled wilderness of the Crau, which keeps guard over the rich harvests of Provence. Not broader than the eye can encompass, its modest expanse yet holds for whosoever is in the mood all the melancholy and *ennui* of the world. Some such emotion was expressed by this simple back-cloth against which, for a moment all too short, the child of indolence and dirt sang one of those plaintive melodies which only a gay-hearted people knows. Mr. Joseph Spurin did this admirably. As his last note died away his impatient lady-love thrust her feather

236

dust-brush into his face. But that is what, metaphorically, all the characters except two had been doing to me throughout the play.

Alas that silly little Mr. Budd should have been so untimely nipped! The play was withdrawn after a week or so. Yet it had seemed to me to ring absolutely true. It was a play about a human being as we know him to be. It forced us to no artificial adjustments because it is " only a play." It was our old friend, a " slice of life " without the unnecessary, morbid assumptions. To the mawkish a slice of life means merely the foretaste of death. Little Mr. Budd seemed to me to ring as true as Tchehov's *Uncle Vanya*, with a truly British difference. No brooding spirit was little Mr. Budd; melancholy had never marked him for her own. He was just an ordinary, common, decent little insurance tout crawling, like the rest of us, between Heaven and earth, but also going joyfully from house to house collecting insurance premiums for the " Ruby," and bringing a streak of sunshine into people's lives. He is not a new character. Mr. Pett Ridge has drawn him a hundred times, Mr. Wells at least thrice—in Kipps, in Mr. Polly, and in the little Cockney, " Bert," who sums up one of the fantasias in the refrain, " It didn't never ought to 'ave 'appened "—Mr. Kipling once in Ortheris, Stevenson once in Huish, who is little Budd gone wrong. Whole regiments of Budd went right in the war and died, as they had lived, in good heart. The play has no plot that matters, it is simply an extravaganza. Yet it is an amusing extravaganza, and the intelligence is not debased in listening to it. I take the scene in which this little Cockney stands

Flights that Failed

at the Palace window and challenges the mob, his heart
in his mouth and just not ducking his head: " If you'll
give me a month's trial as your prince, go home quietly;
if you won't, shoot! " to be as true as anything on the
grandest scale. *Mr. Budd* is the littlest of little plays.
It is not the whole world, it is not even a chrysolite, it is a
little bit of looking-glass entire and perfect in its reflection. From the ridiculous to the sublime is but a step,
and Mr. Tubby Edlin as the comic little tout brings
me to the very verge of tears. By this power of pathos
we know the great comic actor. So little Robson and
Dan Leno; so James Welch, Chaplin, and Mr. Edlin.
The English genius does not run easily to the heroic,
but rather to the heroic in disguise. The Latin would
doubtless have drawn some magnificent cartoon which
we English, biting our lip, would have striven not to find
absurd. One wholly sublime play has been achieved on
this theme of the plain citizen at odds with that tremendous destiny which, to simple souls, admits only of
the simplest solution. That play is Maeterlinck's *The
Burgomaster of Stilemonde*. Sir John Martin Harvey,
shunning the West End as he would revue, gave us at
the Lyceum one or two performances of this masterpiece. His hero and Mr. Maltby's hero are brothers.
Mr. Budd of Kennington, S.E., was obviously not smart
enough for the West End, and I had no illusions about
its prospects. It was not the play which crashed; it
was the public whose visibility was too low.